FREE Study Skills Video

Dear Customer,

Thank you for your purchase from Mometrix! We consider it an honor and a privilege that you have purchased our product and we want to ensure your satisfaction.

As a way of showing our appreciation and to help us better serve you, we have developed Study Skills Videos that we would like to give you for <u>FREE</u>. These videos cover our *best practices* for getting ready for your exam, from how to use our study materials to how to best prepare for the day of the test.

All that we ask is that you email us with feedback that would describe your experience so far with our product. Good, bad, or indifferent, we want to know what you think!

To get your FREE Study Skills Videos, you can use the **QR code** below, or send us an **email** at studyvideos@mometrix.com with *FREE VIDEOS* in the subject line and the following information in the body of the email:

- The name of the product you purchased.
- Your product rating on a scale of 1-5, with 5 being the highest rating.
- Your feedback. It can be long, short, or anything in between. We just want to know your impressions and experience so far with our product. (Good feedback might include how our study material met your needs and ways we might be able to make it even better. You could highlight features that you found helpful or features that you think we should add.)

If you have any questions or concerns, please don't hesitate to contact me directly.

Thanks again!

Sincerely,

Jay Willis
Vice President
jay.willis@mometrix.com
1-800-673-8175

SCAN HERE

Mometrix
TEST PREPARATION
The World's #1 Test Preparation Company

Cosmetology
Exam Secrets
Study Guide

Cosmetology Test Review for the
National Cosmetology
Written Examination

Written and edited by Mometrix Test Prep

Printed in the United States of America

This paper meets the requirements of ANSI/NISO Z39.48-1992 (Permanence of Paper).

Mometrix offers volume discount pricing to institutions. For more information or a price quote, please contact our sales department at sales@mometrix.com or 888-248-1219.

Mometrix Media LLC is not affiliated with or endorsed by any official testing organization. All organizational and test names are trademarks of their respective owners.

Paperback
ISBN 13: 978-1-60971-467-3
ISBN 10: 1-6097-1467-9

DEAR FUTURE EXAM SUCCESS STORY

First of all, **THANK YOU** for purchasing Mometrix study materials!

Second, congratulations! You are one of the few determined test-takers who are committed to doing whatever it takes to excel on your exam. **You have come to the right place.** We developed these study materials with one goal in mind: to deliver you the information you need in a format that's concise and easy to use.

In addition to optimizing your guide for the content of the test, we've outlined our recommended steps for breaking down the preparation process into small, attainable goals so you can make sure you stay on track.

We've also analyzed the entire test-taking process, identifying the most common pitfalls and showing how you can overcome them and be ready for any curveball the test throws you.

Standardized testing is one of the biggest obstacles on your road to success, which only increases the importance of doing well in the high-pressure, high-stakes environment of test day. Your results on this test could have a significant impact on your future, and this guide provides the information and practical advice to help you achieve your full potential on test day.

Your success is our success

We would love to hear from you! If you would like to share the story of your exam success or if you have any questions or comments in regard to our products, please contact us at **800-673-8175** or **support@mometrix.com**.

Thanks again for your business and we wish you continued success!

Sincerely,
The Mometrix Test Preparation Team

Need more help? Check out our flashcards at:
http://mometrixflashcards.com/Cosmetology

TABLE OF CONTENTS

Introduction

Thank you for purchasing this resource! You have made the choice to prepare yourself for a test that could have a huge impact on your future, and this guide is designed to help you be fully ready for test day. Obviously, it's important to have a solid understanding of the test material, but you also need to be prepared for the unique environment and stressors of the test, so that you can perform to the best of your abilities.

For this purpose, the first section that appears in this guide is the **Secret Keys**. We've devoted countless hours to meticulously researching what works and what doesn't, and we've boiled down our findings to the five most impactful steps you can take to improve your performance on the test. We start at the beginning with study planning and move through the preparation process, all the way to the testing strategies that will help you get the most out of what you know when you're finally sitting in front of the test.

We recommend that you start preparing for your test as far in advance as possible. However, if you've bought this guide as a last-minute study resource and only have a few days before your test, we recommend that you skip over the first two Secret Keys since they address a long-term study plan.

If you struggle with **test anxiety**, we strongly encourage you to check out our recommendations for how you can overcome it. Test anxiety is a formidable foe, but it can be beaten, and we want to make sure you have the tools you need to defeat it.

Secret Key #1 – Plan Big, Study Small

There's a lot riding on your performance. If you want to ace this test, you're going to need to keep your skills sharp and the material fresh in your mind. You need a plan that lets you review everything you need to know while still fitting in your schedule. We'll break this strategy down into three categories.

Information Organization

Start with the information you already have: the official test outline. From this, you can make a complete list of all the concepts you need to cover before the test. Organize these concepts into groups that can be studied together, and create a list of any related vocabulary you need to learn so you can brush up on any difficult terms. You'll want to keep this vocabulary list handy once you actually start studying since you may need to add to it along the way.

Time Management

Once you have your set of study concepts, decide how to spread them out over the time you have left before the test. Break your study plan into small, clear goals so you have a manageable task for each day and know exactly what you're doing. Then just focus on one small step at a time. When you manage your time this way, you don't need to spend hours at a time studying. Studying a small block of content for a short period each day helps you retain information better and avoid stressing over how much you have left to do. You can relax knowing that you have a plan to cover everything in time. In order for this strategy to be effective though, you have to start studying early and stick to your schedule. Avoid the exhaustion and futility that comes from last-minute cramming!

Study Environment

The environment you study in has a big impact on your learning. Studying in a coffee shop, while probably more enjoyable, is not likely to be as fruitful as studying in a quiet room. It's important to keep distractions to a minimum. You're only planning to study for a short block of time, so make the most of it. Don't pause to check your phone or get up to find a snack. It's also important to **avoid multitasking**. Research has consistently shown that multitasking will make your studying dramatically less effective. Your study area should also be comfortable and well-lit so you don't have the distraction of straining your eyes or sitting on an uncomfortable chair.

 The time of day you study is also important. You want to be rested and alert. Don't wait until just before bedtime. Study when you'll be most likely to comprehend and remember. Even better, if you know what time of day your test will be, set that time aside for study. That way your brain will be used to working on that subject at that specific time and you'll have a better chance of recalling information.

Finally, it can be helpful to team up with others who are studying for the same test. Your actual studying should be done in as isolated an environment as possible, but the work of organizing the information and setting up the study plan can be divided up. In between study sessions, you can discuss with your teammates the concepts that you're all studying and quiz each other on the details. Just be sure that your teammates are as serious about the test as you are. If you find that your study time is being replaced with social time, you might need to find a new team.

Secret Key #2 – Make Your Studying Count

You're devoting a lot of time and effort to preparing for this test, so you want to be absolutely certain it will pay off. This means doing more than just reading the content and hoping you can remember it on test day. It's important to make every minute of study count. There are two main areas you can focus on to make your studying count.

Retention

It doesn't matter how much time you study if you can't remember the material. You need to make sure you are retaining the concepts. To check your retention of the information you're learning, try recalling it at later times with minimal prompting. Try carrying around flashcards and glance at one or two from time to time or ask a friend who's also studying for the test to quiz you.

To enhance your retention, look for ways to put the information into practice so that you can apply it rather than simply recalling it. If you're using the information in practical ways, it will be much easier to remember. Similarly, it helps to solidify a concept in your mind if you're not only reading it to yourself but also explaining it to someone else. Ask a friend to let you teach them about a concept you're a little shaky on (or speak aloud to an imaginary audience if necessary). As you try to summarize, define, give examples, and answer your friend's questions, you'll understand the concepts better and they will stay with you longer. Finally, step back for a big picture view and ask yourself how each piece of information fits with the whole subject. When you link the different concepts together and see them working together as a whole, it's easier to remember the individual components.

Finally, practice showing your work on any multi-step problems, even if you're just studying. Writing out each step you take to solve a problem will help solidify the process in your mind, and you'll be more likely to remember it during the test.

Modality

Modality simply refers to the means or method by which you study. Choosing a study modality that fits your own individual learning style is crucial. No two people learn best in exactly the same way, so it's important to know your strengths and use them to your advantage.

For example, if you learn best by visualization, focus on visualizing a concept in your mind and draw an image or a diagram. Try color-coding your notes, illustrating them, or creating symbols that will trigger your mind to recall a learned concept. If you learn best by hearing or discussing information, find a study partner who learns the same way or read aloud to yourself. Think about how to put the information in your own words. Imagine that you are giving a lecture on the topic and record yourself so you can listen to it later.

For any learning style, flashcards can be helpful. Organize the information so you can take advantage of spare moments to review. Underline key words or phrases. Use different colors for different categories. Mnemonic devices (such as creating a short list in which every item starts with the same letter) can also help with retention. Find what works best for you and use it to store the information in your mind most effectively and easily.

Secret Key #3 – Practice the Right Way

Your success on test day depends not only on how many hours you put into preparing, but also on whether you prepared the right way. It's good to check along the way to see if your studying is paying off. One of the most effective ways to do this is by taking practice tests to evaluate your progress. Practice tests are useful because they show exactly where you need to improve. Every time you take a practice test, pay special attention to these three groups of questions:

- The questions you got wrong
- The questions you had to guess on, even if you guessed right
- The questions you found difficult or slow to work through

This will show you exactly what your weak areas are, and where you need to devote more study time. Ask yourself why each of these questions gave you trouble. Was it because you didn't understand the material? Was it because you didn't remember the vocabulary? Do you need more repetitions on this type of question to build speed and confidence? Dig into those questions and figure out how you can strengthen your weak areas as you go back to review the material.

 Additionally, many practice tests have a section explaining the answer choices. It can be tempting to read the explanation and think that you now have a good understanding of the concept. However, an explanation likely only covers part of the question's broader context. Even if the explanation makes perfect sense, **go back and investigate** every concept related to the question until you're positive you have a thorough understanding.

As you go along, keep in mind that the practice test is just that: practice. Memorizing these questions and answers will not be very helpful on the actual test because it is unlikely to have any of the same exact questions. If you only know the right answers to the sample questions, you won't be prepared for the real thing. **Study the concepts** until you understand them fully, and then you'll be able to answer any question that shows up on the test.

It's important to wait on the practice tests until you're ready. If you take a test on your first day of study, you may be overwhelmed by the amount of material covered and how much you need to learn. Work up to it gradually.

On test day, you'll need to be prepared for answering questions, managing your time, and using the test-taking strategies you've learned. It's a lot to balance, like a mental marathon that will have a big impact on your future. Like training for a marathon, you'll need to start slowly and work your way up. When test day arrives, you'll be ready.

Start with the strategies you've read in the first two Secret Keys—plan your course and study in the way that works best for you. If you have time, consider using multiple study resources to get different approaches to the same concepts. It can be helpful to see difficult concepts from more than one angle. Then find a good source for practice tests. Many times, the test website will suggest potential study resources or provide sample tests.

4

Practice Test Strategy

If you're able to find at least three practice tests, we recommend this strategy:

Untimed and Open-Book Practice

Take the first test with no time constraints and with your notes and study guide handy. Take your time and focus on applying the strategies you've learned.

Timed and Open-Book Practice

Take the second practice test open-book as well, but set a timer and practice pacing yourself to finish in time.

Timed and Closed-Book Practice

Take any other practice tests as if it were test day. Set a timer and put away your study materials. Sit at a table or desk in a quiet room, imagine yourself at the testing center, and answer questions as quickly and accurately as possible.

Keep repeating timed and closed-book tests on a regular basis until you run out of practice tests or it's time for the actual test. Your mind will be ready for the schedule and stress of test day, and you'll be able to focus on recalling the material you've learned.

Secret Key #4 – Pace Yourself

Once you're fully prepared for the material on the test, your biggest challenge on test day will be managing your time. Just knowing that the clock is ticking can make you panic even if you have plenty of time left. Work on pacing yourself so you can build confidence against the time constraints of the exam. Pacing is a difficult skill to master, especially in a high-pressure environment, so **practice is vital**.

Set time expectations for your pace based on how much time is available. For example, if a section has 60 questions and the time limit is 30 minutes, you know you have to average 30 seconds or less per question in order to answer them all. Although 30 seconds is the hard limit, set 25 seconds per question as your goal, so you reserve extra time to spend on harder questions. When you budget extra time for the harder questions, you no longer have any reason to stress when those questions take longer to answer.

Don't let this time expectation distract you from working through the test at a calm, steady pace, but keep it in mind so you don't spend too much time on any one question. Recognize that taking extra time on one question you don't understand may keep you from answering two that you do understand later in the test. If your time limit for a question is up and you're still not sure of the answer, mark it and move on, and come back to it later if the time and the test format allow. If the testing format doesn't allow you to return to earlier questions, just make an educated guess; then put it out of your mind and move on.

On the easier questions, be careful not to rush. It may seem wise to hurry through them so you have more time for the challenging ones, but it's not worth missing one if you know the concept and just didn't take the time to read the question fully. Work efficiently but make sure you understand the question and have looked at all of the answer choices, since more than one may seem right at first.

Even if you're paying attention to the time, you may find yourself a little behind at some point. You should speed up to get back on track, but do so wisely. Don't panic; just take a few seconds less on each question until you're caught up. Don't guess without thinking, but do look through the answer choices and eliminate any you know are wrong. If you can get down to two choices, it is often worthwhile to guess from those. Once you've chosen an answer, move on and don't dwell on any that you skipped or had to hurry through. If a question was taking too long, chances are it was one of the harder ones, so you weren't as likely to get it right anyway.

On the other hand, if you find yourself getting ahead of schedule, it may be beneficial to slow down a little. The more quickly you work, the more likely you are to make a careless mistake that will affect your score. You've budgeted time for each question, so don't be afraid to spend that time. Practice an efficient but careful pace to get the most out of the time you have.

6

Secret Key #5 – Have a Plan for Guessing

When you're taking the test, you may find yourself stuck on a question. Some of the answer choices seem better than others, but you don't see the one answer choice that is obviously correct. What do you do?

The scenario described above is very common, yet most test takers have not effectively prepared for it. Developing and practicing a plan for guessing may be one of the single most effective uses of your time as you get ready for the exam.

In developing your plan for guessing, there are three questions to address:

- When should you start the guessing process?
- How should you narrow down the choices?
- Which answer should you choose?

When to Start the Guessing Process

Unless your plan for guessing is to select C every time (which, despite its merits, is not what we recommend), you need to leave yourself enough time to apply your answer elimination strategies. Since you have a limited amount of time for each question, that means that if you're going to give yourself the best shot at guessing correctly, you have to decide quickly whether or not you will guess.

Of course, the best-case scenario is that you don't have to guess at all, so first, see if you can answer the question based on your knowledge of the subject and basic reasoning skills. Focus on the key words in the question and try to jog your memory of related topics. Give yourself a chance to bring the knowledge to mind, but once you realize that you don't have (or you can't access) the knowledge you need to answer the question, it's time to start the guessing process.

It's almost always better to start the guessing process too early than too late. It only takes a few seconds to remember something and answer the question from knowledge. Carefully eliminating wrong answer choices takes longer. Plus, going through the process of eliminating answer choices can actually help jog your memory.

Summary: Start the guessing process as soon as you decide that you can't answer the question based on your knowledge.

7

How to Narrow Down the Choices

The next chapter in this book (**Test-Taking Strategies**) includes a wide range of strategies for how to approach questions and how to look for answer choices to eliminate. You will definitely want to read those carefully, practice them, and figure out which ones work best for you. Here though, we're going to address a mindset rather than a particular strategy.

Your odds of guessing an answer correctly depend on how many options you are choosing from.

Number of options left	5	4	3	2	1
Odds of guessing correctly	20%	25%	33%	50%	100%

You can see from this chart just how valuable it is to be able to eliminate incorrect answers and make an educated guess, but there are two things that many test takers do that cause them to miss out on the benefits of guessing:

- Accidentally eliminating the correct answer
- Selecting an answer based on an impression

We'll look at the first one here, and the second one in the next section.

To avoid accidentally eliminating the correct answer, we recommend a thought exercise called **the $5 challenge**. In this challenge, you only eliminate an answer choice from contention if you are willing to bet $5 on it being wrong. Why $5? Five dollars is a small but not insignificant amount of money. It's an amount you could afford to lose but wouldn't want to throw away. And while losing

$5 once might not hurt too much, doing it twenty times will set you back $100. In the same way, each small decision you make—eliminating a choice here, guessing on a question there—won't by itself impact your score very much, but when you put them all together, they can make a big difference. By holding each answer choice elimination decision to a higher standard, you can reduce the risk of accidentally eliminating the correct answer.

The $5 challenge can also be applied in a positive sense: If you are willing to bet $5 that an answer choice *is* correct, go ahead and mark it as correct.

Summary: Only eliminate an answer choice if you are willing to bet $5 that it is wrong.

Which Answer to Choose

You're taking the test. You've run into a hard question and decided you'll have to guess. You've eliminated all the answer choices you're willing to bet $5 on. Now you have to pick an answer. Why do we even need to talk about this? Why can't you just pick whichever one you feel like when the time comes?

The answer to these questions is that if you don't come into the test with a plan, you'll rely on your impression to select an answer choice, and if you do that, you risk falling into a trap. The test writers know that everyone who takes their test will be guessing on some of the questions, so they intentionally write wrong answer choices to seem plausible. You still have to pick an answer though, and if the wrong answer choices are designed to look right, how can you ever be sure that you're not falling for their trap? The best solution we've found to this dilemma is to take the decision out of your hands entirely. Here is the process we recommend:

Once you've eliminated any choices that you are confident (willing to bet $5) are wrong, select the first remaining choice as your answer.

Whether you choose to select the first remaining choice, the second, or the last, the important thing is that you use some preselected standard. Using this approach guarantees that you will not be enticed into selecting an answer choice that looks right, because you are not basing your decision on how the answer choices look.

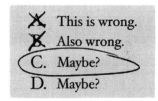

This is not meant to make you question your knowledge. Instead, it is to help you recognize the difference between your knowledge and your impressions. There's a huge difference between thinking an answer is right because of what you know, and thinking an answer is right because it looks or sounds like it should be right.

Summary: To ensure that your selection is appropriately random, make a predetermined selection from among all answer choices you have not eliminated.

Test-Taking Strategies

This section contains a list of test-taking strategies that you may find helpful as you work through the test. By taking what you know and applying logical thought, you can maximize your chances of answering any question correctly!

It is very important to realize that every question is different and every person is different: no single strategy will work on every question, and no single strategy will work for every person. That's why we've included all of them here, so you can try them out and determine which ones work best for different types of questions and which ones work best for you.

Question Strategies

⊘ READ CAREFULLY

Read the question and the answer choices carefully. Don't miss the question because you misread the terms. You have plenty of time to read each question thoroughly and make sure you understand what is being asked. Yet a happy medium must be attained, so don't waste too much time. You must read carefully and efficiently.

⊘ CONTEXTUAL CLUES

Look for contextual clues. If the question includes a word you are not familiar with, look at the immediate context for some indication of what the word might mean. Contextual clues can often give you all the information you need to decipher the meaning of an unfamiliar word. Even if you can't determine the meaning, you may be able to narrow down the possibilities enough to make a solid guess at the answer to the question.

⊘ PREFIXES

If you're having trouble with a word in the question or answer choices, try dissecting it. Take advantage of every clue that the word might include. Prefixes and suffixes can be a huge help. Usually, they allow you to determine a basic meaning. *Pre-* means before, *post-* means after, *pro-* is positive, *de-* is negative. From prefixes and suffixes, you can get an idea of the general meaning of the word and try to put it into context.

⊘ HEDGE WORDS

Watch out for critical hedge words, such as *likely, may, can, sometimes, often, almost, mostly, usually, generally, rarely,* and *sometimes.* Question writers insert these hedge phrases to cover every possibility. Often an answer choice will be wrong simply because it leaves no room for exception. Be on guard for answer choices that have definitive words such as *exactly* and *always.*

⊘ SWITCHBACK WORDS

Stay alert for *switchbacks.* These are the words and phrases frequently used to alert you to shifts in thought. The most common switchback words are *but, although,* and *however.* Others include *nevertheless, on the other hand, even though, while, in spite of, despite,* and *regardless of.* Switchback words are important to catch because they can change the direction of the question or an answer choice.

10

⊘ FACE VALUE

When in doubt, use common sense. Accept the situation in the problem at face value. Don't read too much into it. These problems will not require you to make wild assumptions. If you have to go beyond creativity and warp time or space in order to have an answer choice fit the question, then you should move on and consider the other answer choices. These are normal problems rooted in reality. The applicable relationship or explanation may not be readily apparent, but it is there for you to figure out. Use your common sense to interpret anything that isn't clear.

Answer Choice Strategies

⊘ ANSWER SELECTION

The most thorough way to pick an answer choice is to identify and eliminate wrong answers until only one is left, then confirm it is the correct answer. Sometimes an answer choice may immediately seem right, but be careful. The test writers will usually put more than one reasonable answer choice on each question, so take a second to read all of them and make sure that the other choices are not equally obvious. As long as you have time left, it is better to read every answer choice than to pick the first one that looks right without checking the others.

⊘ ANSWER CHOICE FAMILIES

An answer choice family consists of two (in rare cases, three) answer choices that are very similar in construction and cannot all be true at the same time. If you see two answer choices that are direct opposites or parallels, one of them is usually the correct answer. For instance, if one answer choice says that quantity x increases and another either says that quantity x decreases (opposite) or says that quantity y increases (parallel), then those answer choices would fall into the same family. An answer choice that doesn't match the construction of the answer choice family is more likely to be incorrect. Most questions will not have answer choice families, but when they do appear, you should be prepared to recognize them.

⊘ ELIMINATE ANSWERS

Eliminate answer choices as soon as you realize they are wrong, but make sure you consider all possibilities. If you are eliminating answer choices and realize that the last one you are left with is also wrong, don't panic. Start over and consider each choice again. There may be something you missed the first time that you will realize on the second pass.

⊘ AVOID FACT TRAPS

Don't be distracted by an answer choice that is factually true but doesn't answer the question. You are looking for the choice that answers the question. Stay focused on what the question is asking for so you don't accidentally pick an answer that is true but incorrect. Always go back to the question and make sure the answer choice you've selected actually answers the question and is not merely a true statement.

⊘ EXTREME STATEMENTS

In general, you should avoid answers that put forth extreme actions as standard practice or proclaim controversial ideas as established fact. An answer choice that states the "process should be used in certain situations, if…" is much more likely to be correct than one that states the "process should be discontinued completely." The first is a calm rational statement and doesn't even make a definitive, uncompromising stance, using a hedge word *if* to provide wiggle room, whereas the second choice is far more extreme.

⊘ BENCHMARK

As you read through the answer choices and you come across one that seems to answer the question well, mentally select that answer choice. This is not your final answer, but it's the one that will help you evaluate the other answer choices. The one that you selected is your benchmark or standard for judging each of the other answer choices. Every other answer choice must be compared to your benchmark. That choice is correct until proven otherwise by another answer choice beating it. If you find a better answer, then that one becomes your new benchmark. Once you've decided that no other choice answers the question as well as your benchmark, you have your final answer.

⊘ PREDICT THE ANSWER

Before you even start looking at the answer choices, it is often best to try to predict the answer. When you come up with the answer on your own, it is easier to avoid distractions and traps because you will know exactly what to look for. The right answer choice is unlikely to be word-for-word what you came up with, but it should be a close match. Even if you are confident that you have the right answer, you should still take the time to read each option before moving on.

General Strategies

⊘ TOUGH QUESTIONS

If you are stumped on a problem or it appears too hard or too difficult, don't waste time. Move on! Remember though, if you can quickly check for obviously incorrect answer choices, your chances of guessing correctly are greatly improved. Before you completely give up, at least try to knock out a couple of possible answers. Eliminate what you can and then guess at the remaining answer choices before moving on.

⊘ CHECK YOUR WORK

Since you will probably not know every term listed and the answer to every question, it is important that you get credit for the ones that you do know. Don't miss any questions through careless mistakes. If at all possible, try to take a second to look back over your answer selection and make sure you've selected the correct answer choice and haven't made a costly careless mistake (such as marking an answer choice that you didn't mean to mark). This quick double check should more than pay for itself in caught mistakes for the time it costs.

⊘ PACE YOURSELF

It's easy to be overwhelmed when you're looking at a page full of questions; your mind is confused and full of random thoughts, and the clock is ticking down faster than you would like. Calm down and maintain the pace that you have set for yourself. Especially as you get down to the last few minutes of the test, don't let the small numbers on the clock make you panic. As long as you are on track by monitoring your pace, you are guaranteed to have time for each question.

⊘ DON'T RUSH

It is very easy to make errors when you are in a hurry. Maintaining a fast pace in answering questions is pointless if it makes you miss questions that you would have gotten right otherwise. Test writers like to include distracting information and wrong answers that seem right. Taking a little extra time to avoid careless mistakes can make all the difference in your test score. Find a pace that allows you to be confident in the answers that you select.

⊘ KEEP MOVING

Panicking will not help you pass the test, so do your best to stay calm and keep moving. Taking deep breaths and going through the answer elimination steps you practiced can help to break through a stress barrier and keep your pace.

Final Notes

The combination of a solid foundation of content knowledge and the confidence that comes from practicing your plan for applying that knowledge is the key to maximizing your performance on test day. As your foundation of content knowledge is built up and strengthened, you'll find that the strategies included in this chapter become more and more effective in helping you quickly sift through the distractions and traps of the test to isolate the correct answer.

Now that you're preparing to move forward into the test content chapters of this book, be sure to keep your goal in mind. As you read, think about how you will be able to apply this information on the test. If you've already seen sample questions for the test and you have an idea of the question format and style, try to come up with questions of your own that you can answer based on what you're reading. This will give you valuable practice applying your knowledge in the same ways you can expect to on test day.

Good luck and good studying!

Cosmetology

General Review

CLEANING HAIR CARE INSTRUMENTS

Apply dry heat at 338° Fahrenheit (170° Celsius) for no less than 60 minutes.

Soak in a Sodium Hypochlorite solution consisting of 200 parts per million of chlorine for no less than 2 minutes.

Soak in Formalin in 10% solution for no less than 20 minutes.

Soak in quaternary ammonium solutions of 1,000 parts per million for no less than 10 minutes.

Soak in 70% alcohol solution for no less than 20 minutes.

Boil at 212° Fahrenheit (100° Celsius) for no less than 15 minutes.

Sterilize by steam at 15 lb (1 atmosphere) pressure at 248° Fahrenheit (120° Celsius) for no less than 30 minutes.

Saturate in approved germicidal oils for clippers and clipper heads and approved germicidal powders for brushes.

WORK SPACE SANITATION

All linens shall be stored in airtight, closed cabinets and properly covered containers with appropriate sanitizing agents and kept apart from other storage areas. Linens will be laundered and sanitized after each client and with a disinfecting solution regularly, and each place of business will have ample amounts of linen for such use. All equipment will be cleaned, disinfected, and stored in a clean, closed drawer or cabinet with the appropriate sanitizing agents. Solutions will be changed regularly to avoid becoming infected, and all sterilizing equipment will be well maintained at all times.

The cover for the headrest shall be changed for each client, and the towels or covers used will also be cleaned or thrown away. Disposable items such as emery boards and permanent wave end papers shall be thrown away immediately after use, and the floor of the work space shall be swept clean after each client.

HAIR PIECE STORAGE AND CLEANING

All hairpieces or wigs, whether for sale, rent, or display, will be kept in dry, sanitary conditions and stored in separated areas to avoid contamination from other hairpieces or necessary equipment. Soiled or unsanitized hairpieces or wigs will be stored separately from all other accoutrement prior to cleaning or maintaining. Any client interested in trying on a hairpiece or wig will cover his/her head with a protective cap, which will be either cleaned immediately after or thrown away. No establishment will offer a hairpiece or wig for sale unless the manufacturing label is still attached or visible, and all hairpieces will be thoroughly cleaned before being resold, rented, or displayed.

HYGIENIC DUTIES

All workers will maintain good personal hygiene and clean outer garments and adhere to exceptional hygiene practices at the workplace. Each worker will wash his or her hands thoroughly after each client and as necessary during the day, especially after eating, smoking, or going to the bathroom. Smoking by any worker is prohibited at the establishment. Combs and other items for use will not be stored in any worker's pocket during the course of the client's visit, and no worker will attempt to remove skin growths or treat skin diseases of any client. Clients with certain conditions such as lice or ringworm will not be treated while afflicted, and no worker with a communicable disease shall perform work-related duties while afflicted.

ELECTRIC AND ELECTROLYSIS INSTRUMENTS

Disinfect such items as clippers or vibrators before each use by removing any unnecessary articles of matter and then thoroughly cleaning the clippers or vibrators with an EPA-approved solution with verified bactericidal, virucidal, or fungicidal activity per the manufacturer's directions. Once these items are disinfected, they may be stored in a clean, covered place for future use.

Before use of an electrolysis instrument on a client, remove the tweezer or needle from the electrolysis instrument and sterilize the tweezer or needle with a steam sterilizer or dry heat sterilizer, both as listed with the FDA and according to the manufacturer's directions. Check the sterilization equipment frequently to determine that the required temperature for sterilization is being reached. If the needle involved is a sterile disposable epilation needle, then manual sterilization is unnecessary, and the needle can be thrown away immediately after use.

ANTIBACTERIAL

Antibacterial is able to kill bacteria and prevent future bacterial growth with the active ingredient of triclosan. Triclosan kills bacteria as well as human growth cells. Possible side effect of antibacterial solutions is the development of resistant bacteria, or "superbugs," and results show that antibacterial products offer little help in killing germs.

ANTISEPTIC AND ASEPTIC

Both terms originally referred to preventing sepsis, or blood poisoning, but now are used to describe preventing microbial impurities from occurring during specialized situations, such as medical operations and the creation of sterile instruments.

PATHOGENIC

Pathogenic means disease causing. Bacteria can be harmful to one person or an entire group of people depending on the specific type of bacteria and can cause diverse diseases, such as tooth pain, diarrhea, and cancer.

RESPIRATORY SYSTEM

When breathing, each person inhales oxygen, which is needed to enrich the blood and provide appropriate nutrients to different parts of the body, and exhales carbon dioxide.

The oxygen travels in through the mouth and nose and moves through the larynx (or "voicebox") and trachea to the chest, where it enters two tubes called the bronchi. The bronchial tubes lead to the lungs, which contain tiny air sacs called alveoli. From there, oxygen diffuses through capillaries into the arterial blood while the carbon dioxide is diffused from the oxygen-depleted blood to the alveoli and released when a person exhales. The diaphragm, a shelf of muscles at the bottom of chest cavity, helps remove the carbon dioxide from the lungs and pull the oxygen into the lungs by

contracting and relaxing during each breath. When a person breathes in, the diaphragm contracts; when a person breathes out, the diaphragm relaxes.

> **Review Video: <u>Respiratory System</u>**
> Visit mometrix.com/academy and enter code: 783075

CARBON DIOXIDE

Carbon dioxide is an atmospheric gas made up of one carbon atom and two oxygen atoms; solid form is called dry ice. Carbon dioxide is obtained from earth movement resulting in gas release, the burning of organic material, and respiration of animals and is utilized by plants during photosynthesis.

OXYGEN

Oxygen is the element utilized by most organisms on Earth and accounts for two-thirds of the human body and nine-tenths of water. Oxygen is highly combustible and very reactive with other elements while being imperative for plant and animal life.

NITROGEN

Nitrogen is the element comprising 78% of the atmosphere and is colorless, odorless, and seemingly lifeless. Used in foods, fertilizer, and explosives, nitrogen can combine with magnesium, lithium, calcium, and oxygen and is an important part of the process of creating ammonia.

NATURAL IMMUNITY

Natural immunity is a barrier to disease and infection; created by the skin, normal bodily secretions, helpful microorganisms, and a working respiratory system. Some people are genetically predisposed toward fighting certain infections or are in the habit of eating a proper diet that fights off disease. Natural immunity can be weakened by a person's stress levels or diet and can cause the body to decrease the natural secretions which leaves the respiratory and digestive systems vulnerable to infection.

ACQUIRED IMMUNITY

Acquired immunity is the result of vaccination. Different vaccines can trigger a body to respond to disease-causing bacteria and increase the body's resistance. The pathogen, or microorganism that causes disease, can be protected against for months or years at a time, depending on the vaccination.

Both types of immunity work together to keep a body as protected against diseases as possible and form an intricate pattern of cells and tissues that interact to maintain good health.

PHYSIOLOGY

Physiology is the study of life functions. As a subgroup of biology, physiology analyzes the functions of everyday existence, such as the growth of a body, the development of muscles or tissues, and the existence of different types of cells. The study includes a focus on the physical aspects of existence, such as birth, growth, consumption of food, waste removals, as well as the chemical processes that occur in the brain and body as related to social interactions, recognition of hierarchies, and memory functions. Physiology includes the study of how each part of the body works on its own and in conjunction with other organs and tissues. The interworkings of the respiratory and digestive systems and the combined results when added to the workings of the nervous system offer the physiologist a more complete understanding of how the body works as a collective whole.

OSHA

The goal of OSHA is to establish certain safety and health requirements for workers at any place of business, provide education and training, and promote improvements in the safety and health of each workplace. OSHA employs around 2,100 inspection specialists, engineers, discrimination investigators, and other technical employees in offices nationwide. The OSHA staff enforces the standards set forth by the organization and acts as a consulting service for many places of business, providing technical support if necessary. Management commitment is the best way for OSHA requirements and guidelines to be adopted in any workplace and implemented by the employees. Different on-site inspections and random polls taken by OSHA specialists have contributed to the requirements for safety and health issues in today's workplace, and improvements are always being made to better serve employees and their employers.

As part of the Department of Labor, OSHA requirements affect almost every worker in the country, specifically those who fall under the following categories: law, academics, occupational health and safety, and journalism. The following occupations are not under the jurisdiction of OSHA: self-employed workers, miners, many public workers, and transportation workers. Through inspections and small focus groups created to ascertain the needs of today's worker, OSHA can continue to improve the basic tenets for the safety and health environments in the workplace. OSHA has made allowances for study into various emerging branches of employees with increasingly obvious requirements for safety and health issues, such as construction workers, and has provided room for criticisms and critiques to better improve the working environment for the worker.

PREVENTING INFECTION

The best way to prevent the spread of infection is to keep the work area clean. Disease-causing microorganisms cannot exist in a clean environment but require warm areas that are moist and unsanitary. Workers should always wash the instruments involved in each particular task as well their own hands between clients or even during the session as needed. Each area should be adequately ventilated to prevent the growth and spread of mold as many people are sensitive to this kind of development and may exhibit respiratory symptoms. The humidity levels should be kept low to preclude any kind of unhealthy growth or infestation, and all surfaces should be kept clean and dry.

CHILDREN

Small children can carry disease-causing microorganisms easily since their immune systems have not been able to build up any kind of resistance to common germs. Daycare centers and schools are logical places for the spreading of such infectious diseases. The children's areas should be well maintained and disinfected, as well as the bathrooms and changing areas. Workers should pay close attention to frequent hand-washing and instrument sterilization between clients and even throughout the interaction.

SENIORS

Senior citizens often have weaker immune systems, which allows their bodies to more easily transmit infectious diseases among assisted-care or nursing home residents and visitors. While many of these adult centers make concession for a regimented cleaning schedule, workers can also adhere to frequent hand-washing and instrument sterilization for their own protection against germs.

COMMON COLD AND FLU

More than 200 different viruses can cause the symptoms for the common cold, such as sneezing, runny nose, cough, and sore throat. The most common disease in the world, the common cold usually lasts about a week for most sufferers. The flu often includes a headache, major muscle aches, fever, and a bad cough. The strain for influenza continues to evolve, and there have been almost 20,000 cases of death involving the flu in this country each year.

There is no known cure for the common cold, but there are several medications available to ease the symptoms. The common cold may develop into secondary bacterial infections of the lungs or sinuses and require antibiotic treatment. Vaccines are the best course of action for flu-sufferers since antibiotics do not cure viruses. However, antibiotics can be used to help a flu-sufferer with any secondary infection resulting from the flu, such as bacterial pneumonia.

Fungal Nail Infections

Fingernails and toenails are breeding grounds for certain microorganisms that thrive in warm, moist environments. Varieties of fungi live under the pink part of the nail and feed on the protein there. The nail becomes thicker, may turn yellow-brown, and have an unpleasant odor from the pus building up underneath the nail. Daily cleansing and some creams or powders may correct the infection, but some more serious infections require oral medication, directly applied medication, or even removal of the nail.

Fungal nail infections can be prevented by the following steps: wash and dry hands and feet completely, wear shower shoes in public water areas, clip toenails and fingernails straight across, wear cotton or wool socks and gloves, use talcum powder, wear comfortable shoes, and avoid nail polish.

Skeletal System

The skeletal system gives the human body its shape, supports interior organs, protects muscles and tissues, allows for movement, produces blood, and stores minerals for survival through the 206 bones that act as a frame for the major organs and tissues of the body. The human skeleton is composed of two parts, which are the axial skeleton and the appendicular skeleton. The axial skeleton includes the skull, sternum, ribs, and vertebral column, while the appendicular skeleton includes the upper extremities, lower extremities, shoulder girdle, and pelvic girdle. The skeleton serves as a protective device for the brain, the heart, and the lungs and is held together through ligaments and tendons and meet at joints.

> **Review Video: Skeletal System**
> Visit mometrix.com/academy and enter code: 256447

MOVEMENT

The skeleton of the human body allows for movement because of the interaction of the muscular system and the skeletal system, usually referred to as the musculo-skeletal system due to their connectivity. Muscles are connected to each other by tendons, which are strong bands or cords of tissue, and the tendons are connected to each other by ligaments, short bands of tough and flexible tissue. The intersection of two bones is called a joint, or articulation, and the subsequent movement is controlled by the contracting and relaxing of the muscles attached. When the elbow bends, the biceps contract and the triceps relax. When the arm straightens, the triceps contact and the biceps relax.

JOINT TYPES

The three types of joints in the human body are classified by the amount of movement they perform. Immovable joints, known as synarthroses, are closely aligned and separated by a thin layer of fibrous connective tissue. The bones in the skull are immovable joints.

Slightly movable joints, known as amphiarthroses, are defined by their connection of hyaline, or fibro, cartilage. The ribs connecting to the sternum are slightly movable joints as they complement the expansion and deflation of the lungs.

Freely movable joints, known as diarthrosis joints, account for most of the joints in the human body. The six types of freely movable joints are the ball-and-socket, condyloid, saddle, pivot, hinge, and gliding.

BALL-AND-SOCKET

Ball-and-socket joints-the ball- or round-shaped end of one bone fits into the cup shaped socket of the other bone, which allows for the greatest range of movement; shoulder and hip

CONDYLOID

Condyloid-oval or egg-shaped bone fits into the oval cavity of the other bone, which allows for angular motion but no rotation; bones in the hand and finger.

SADDLE

Saddle is where both bones have convex and concave parts, which allows for a wide range of motion; thumb only.

PIVOT

Pivot are rounded surfaces of one bone fit into a ring, which allows rotation; neck.

HINGE

Hinge is the projection of one bone fits into depression of another, which allows extension; elbow, knee.

GLIDING JOINTS

Gliding is when the flat surface of one bone moves against flat surface of another, which allows for sliding; carpals in the wrist.

BLOOD PRODUCTION

The skeleton is important in the production of blood and storing of minerals. The marrow located in some of the bones produces red blood cells. Red blood cells are produced at an average of 2.6 million each second. The newly created red blood cells replace the older blood cells used by the liver.

STORING MINERALS

Bones store minerals needed for survival, such as phosphorous and calcium. If the bones store excessive amounts of these minerals, there is a build up within the bones themselves and can be noticeable especially at the top of the bent knee or at the elbow. When the diet fails to provide these nutrients to the blood, the body will withdraw from the bones so that the quality of the blood remains consistent.

SKULL

The skull is made up of eight cranial and fourteen facial bones and acts as the bony frame for the head. The eight cranial bones are:

- frontal, which forms part of the cranial cavity, forehead, brow ridges, and nasal cavity
- left and right parietal, which form the majority of the superior and lateral portions

- left and right temporal, which form the lateral walls and house the external ear
- occipital, which forms the posterior and inferior portions and acts as the joint or articulation for the neck
- phenoid, which forms part of the eye socket and the skull bottom
- ethmoid, which forms the medial portions of the eye sockets and the roof of the nasal cavity

FACIAL BONES

The facial bones of the skull comprise the upper and lower jaw and other facets of the face. The fourteen bones are the:

- mandible, or lower jawbone, which is the only freely moving joint in the head
- left and right maxilla, which form part of the roof of the mouth, the nose, and eye sockets
- left and right palatine, which forms part of the nasal cavity and posterior part of the roof of the mouth
- left and right zygomatic, or cheek bones, which form part of the eye sockets
- left and right nasal, which form the superior part of the bridge of the nose
- left and right lacrimal, which form part of the eye sockets
- vomer, which forms part of the nasal septum, or divider between the nostrils
- left and right inferior turbinate, which forms the lateral walls of the nose

STERNUM

A flat and almost dagger shaped bone; the sternum is located in the middle front of the chest cavity. The sternum and ribs form the rib cage that protects the heart, lungs, and major blood vessels and is made up of three parts:

1. the manubrim, or "handle," which is located at the top of the sternum and is connected to the first two ribs
2. the body, or "blade" or "gladiolus," which is located at the middle and connects the third to seventh ribs with indirect connection to the eighth rib
3. the xiphoid process, or "tip," which is located at the bottom and transitions from cartilage to bone in the later years of life

The three segments usually fuse in adult years.

RIBS

Ribs are flat, thin, curved bones forming a cage around the vital organs of the upper body and are made up of 24 bones in 12 pairs. The first seven pairs of bones are called true ribs and are connected to the sternum by strips of cartilage, or "costal cartilage," and to the spine in back. The next three pairs of bones are slightly shorter and only connected to the seventh rib and the spine. These three pairs are called false ribs since they do not connect to the sternum in the front. The last two pairs of ribs are called floating ribs since they are the smallest of the rib bones and are connected to the spine but not any front ribs or the sternum. Ribs protect the heart and lungs and also parts of the stomach and kidneys, and ribs give the chest its shape.

SPINE

Also called the vertebral column or backbone, the spine consists of 33 irregularly shaped bones, called vertebrae, which are divided into five categories:

4. The cervical vertebrae, the first seven bones, form the flexible framework for the neck, providing head support and neck movement
5. The first vertebra is called the atlas, and the second is the axis. The thoracic vertebrae, the next twelve bones, form the back of the rib cage, increasing in size from top to bottom
6. The lumbar vertebrae, the next five bones, are the largest and support most of the body's weight
7. The sacrum, the next four or five bones dependent on age, forms the back of the pelvic girdle. After about age 26, the bones fuse together
8. The coccyx, the last three to five bones which are fused together for adults, is the bottom of the spine and connects to many muscles

MOVEMENT

The bones of the spine or vertebral column are interspersed with intervertebral discs that are made of fibrous cartilage and act as shock absorbers. These discs compress with age and result in a loss of height for seniors. Four separate curves allow human beings to stand straight and maintain balance. These curves are the cervical curve, thoracic curve, lumbar curve, and pelvic or sacral curve. The cervical curve forms at around 3 months when a baby starts to hold up its head, and the lumbar curve develops when a child learns to walk. The spine supports the head and arms and is attached to many muscles in the back while protecting the spinal cord, a network of nerves that controls many functions in the body.

ARM

The arm, or brachium, refers to the part of the body between the shoulder and elbow. This bone is called the humerus and is the longest bone in the upper extremity. The top of the humerus is large and rounded to fit into the scapula at the shoulder. Two depressions exist at the bottom of the humerus to allow for connection to the ulna and radius of the forearm. The radius connects to the arm on the lateral side, or away from the body, and the ulna connects to the arm on the medial side, or close to the body. The ulna and radius comprise the elbow. The ulnar nerve, or "funny bone," is protected by the bottom of the humerus.

FOREARM

The forearm refers to the part of the body between the elbow and wrist and is formed by two bones, the radius and the ulna. The radius is shorter and thicker than the ulna, and the radius connects to the elbow on the lateral side or away from the body. The ulna is more firmly connected to the humerus and connects on the medial side or closer to the body. The radius is the more active component in the movements of the wrist and the hand, and the radius crosses over the ulna when the palm of the hand is turned down. The radius and ulna connect to the humerus at the top and to the wrist at the bottom.

HAND

Made up of three parts and only 27 bones, the hand is one of the most active parts of the body. The wrist, or carpus, is made up of 8 small bones called carpal bones that are connected by ligaments, and these bones are arranged in two rows of four. The top row, closer to the forearm, from the thumb or lateral side to the medial side is made up of the scaphoid, lunate, triquetral, and pisiform bones. The second row, closest to the fingers, from lateral to medial side contains the trapezium,

trapezoid, capitate, and hamate bones. The scaphoid and lunate form the connection to the bottom of the radius.

PALM AND FINGERS

The fleshy inside part of the hand, or palm, is called the metacarpus and is made up of five metacarpal bones that are each aligned with a finger. These bones are numbered I to V beginning at the thumb. The base of these bones connects to the wrist, and the top connects to the fingers. The tops of these bones form the knuckles.

The fingers are comprised of 14 bones or phalanges, and one section is called a phalanx. Phalanges are arranged in three rows: the proximal row is closest to the metacarpals, the middle row is in the center, and the distal row is the furthest from the metacarpals. Each finger has a proximal, middle, and distal phalanx, but the thumb or pollex has only the proximal phalanx and distal phalanx.

THIGH

The thigh refers to the area between hip and knee and is made up of the femur. The femur or thighbone is the longest and largest bone in the human body and often the strongest due to size and mineral storage.

LEG

The leg refers to the area between the knee and ankle and is formed by the fibula on the lateral side, or away from the body, and the tibia on the medial side, or closer to the body. The tibia is also referred to as the shinbone and connects to the femur at the knee joint. The tibia is larger than the fibula as it sustains most of the body weight, while the fibula acts as the point for the muscles to attach.

PATELLA

The patella, or "kneecap," is the large bone between the femur and tibia that protects the knee joint and strengthens the tendon forming the knee.

FOOT

Containing 26 bones of the ankle, instep, and five toes, the foot or pes is the last of the lower extremities. The ankle or tarsus is made up of 7 tarsal bones which are similar in form and function to the bones in the wrist. The largest tarsal bone is the calcaneus or heel bone and serves as a base for the talus to connect to the tibia. This connection between the talus and tibia permits the ankle to extend and flex. The navicular bone is in front of the talus, and the bones of the foot are the medial, intermediate, lateral cuneiform, and cuboid bones arranged from medial, closer to the body, to lateral, away from the body.

The metatarsal bones or phalanges of the foot are similar in position and number to the fingers. From the big toe on the medial side, the five bones are numbered I to V. The first metatarsal bone is larger than the others because it helps maintain body weight and balance. The 14 phalanges of the foot are arranged similarly with the hand in the proximal row, the middle row, and the distal row. The big toe or hallux only has a proximal and distal phalanx. The two arches are formed by the structure and arrangement of the bones, and their shape is maintained by the tendons and ligaments. Arches can fall due to weakening of tendons and ligaments in the foot but normally just give some when weight is applied and return to normal shape when weight is removed.

23

SHOULDER GIRDLE

The shoulder girdle or pectoral girdle comprises the two clavicles and two scapulae. The clavicle, or "collarbone," is a slender bone connecting the upper arm to the chest and allows the shoulder joint more freedom of movement by supporting it away from the body. The ends of the clavicle connect to the scapula and the sternum.

The scapula, or "shoulder blade," is a large, flat bone located at the back of the rib cage and overlays the top seven ribs. The scapula has a shallow depression called the glenoid cavity that forms the joint with the top of the humerus.

The main function of the shoulder girdle is to act as an attachment for numerous muscles that control the shoulder and elbow joints and connects the upper extremities to the axial skeleton.

PELVIC GIRDLE

The pelvic girdle or hip girdle is made up of two coxal or hip bones. Each coxal bone consists of three parts for children: the ilium, ischium, and pubis. In adulthood, these three bones fuse into a single bone. In the back, these coxal bones meet at the sacrum and are connected by the pubic symphysis in the front. The pelvic girdle supports the weight of the vertebral column and protects the lower organs such as the bladder, reproductive organs, and a developing fetus in pregnant women.

The pelvic girdle is more massive in men with the iliac crests closer together. In women, the pelvic girdle is more delicate with the iliac crests farther apart for the birthing process. When the iliac crests are too close together for a baby to pass through the woman's pelvis, a cesarean section may be performed.

BONE TYPES

The human body consists of several different bones which are classified into four categories: long, short, flat, and irregular.

Long bones work as levers and are longer than they are wide. Examples of this type include the humerus, ulna, femur, and tibia.

Short bones are cube shaped and found in the wrists and ankles.

Flat bones have large surfaces to protect organs and muscle attachment. Examples of this type include the cranial bones, scapulae, and ribs.

Irregular bones refer to all the other bones that do not qualify for the first three types since they have different sizes, shapes, and features. Examples of this type include vertebrae and some skull bones.

BONE COMPOSITION

All bones are made up of tissue that comes in two kinds or forms: compact or dense tissue and spongy or cancellous tissue. Compact or dense tissue is a hard tissue that forms the protective covering of all bones. Spongy or cancellous tissue occurs inside most bones and is not as easily viewed as compact bone tissue. The bone tissue is made up of five different types of bone cells, such as osteogenic, osteoblast, osteocyte, osteoclast, and bone-lining, and is contained in a mass of minerals or inorganic salts such as phosphorus or calcium. These minerals give the bones their strength, and the ground substance and collagenous fibers give the bones more range and flexibility.

The five types of bone cells are:

9. Osteogenic-cells that respond to breakage or trauma by creating bone-forming or bone-destroying cells
10. Osteoblast-cells in the high metabolism areas of the bone that use unmineralized ground substance for bone-forming
11. Osteocyte-cells made from osteoblasts that have formed the bone tissue around themselves and maintain the health of the bone tissue by determining the quality of the bone mineral content and the amount of calcium released from the bone to the blood
12. Osteoclast-cells large enough to break down bone tissue that assist in growth, repair, and reforming
13. Bone-lining-cells made from osteoblasts at the surface of the bones of most adults and are believed to control the movement of phosphate and calcium in and out of the bone

MUSCULAR SYSTEM

As the part of the body allowing for movement, muscles contribute to almost half the weight of the human body and are bundles of cells and fiber. Controlled by the brain, muscles are attached to bones by tendons, stretchy cords of tissue, and contract or relax which causes bodily movement. The more than 640 muscles rarely work alone but act in conjunction with other muscles. For example, the forearm is raised by flexing the bicep and relaxing the tricep and then lowered by flexing the tricep and relaxing the bicep. Muscles cannot push, so the arrangement of muscles in opposing teams allows for this ability to adjust and readjust. Muscles work together in muscle groups and are classified as either voluntary or involuntary.

> **Review Video: Muscular System**
> Visit mometrix.com/academy and enter code: 967216

VOLUNTARY MUSCLES

Voluntary muscles are controlled by thoughts and moved at will by the individual. The brain converts protein to chemical energy and sends messages along the nervous system, which causes the muscle group to respond by flexing or relaxing depending on the kind of movement desired by the individual. Voluntary muscles include facial muscles, arms, fingers, and legs.

INVOLUNTARY MUSCLES

Involuntary muscles are controlled by the brain on another level. These movements occur without conscious thought and cannot be paused for long periods of time if at all. Such involuntary muscles include the heart, the liver, the stomach, and the intestines.

While voluntary muscles allow people to express themselves or complete a specific task, involuntary muscles contribute to the survival of the human body and continue on the course of maintaining and growing in response to all other outside stimuli.

MUSCLE TISSUE

There are three types of muscle tissue: cardiac, skeletal, and smooth. Cardiac muscle tissue is striated and contracts or shortens by way of the sliding filament method. Cardiac muscles make up the brain and wall of the heart or mydocardium. Cardiac muscle tissue forms branching fibers that are attached together and not directly to a bone. Skeletal muscle tissue contributes almost 40% of the body weight of an adult and is also striated. These long muscle fibers are each cells containing several nuclei. The nervous system controls the movement of these tissues, and, while most skeletal muscle contractions are involuntary, the skeletal muscle tissue is still classified as voluntary.

Smooth muscle tissue makes up most of the internal organs, such as arteries, veins, and bladder, and are also controlled by the nervous as well as hormones. Smooth muscles are classified as involuntary.

MAJOR SKELETAL MUSCLES

There are six major skeletal muscle groups: deltoid, pectoralis, rectus abdominis, biceps/triceps, quadriceps, and gluteus maximus. The deltoid is located at the shoulders and helps in such movements as shrugging or swinging a bat. The pectoralis, or "pectorals" or "pecs," is located at each side of the chest and may become more pronounced in men who lift weights. The rectus abdominis, or "abdominals" or "abs," is the muscle under the rib cage that allows a person to sit up. The bicep/tricep pairing is located on the upper arm and allows for lifting. The quadriceps, or "quads," is located at the front of the thigh and helps in walking or running. The gluteus maximus is located at the rear and helps in walking and other aerobic exercise.

FACIAL MUSCLES

The facial muscles are the most indicative of how a person feels and show the most in regards to age and health. Facial muscles do not attach directly to the facial bones but rest on them and attach under the skin. This placement of muscles allows for different facial expressions with only the difference in a couple of muscle contractions. The tongue is an important part of the facial muscles but is actually its own group of muscles. The back part of the tongue is attached by the frenulum, a thin membrane, to the bottom of the mouth. The front part of the tongue moves around a lot and assists in creating speech. The muscles in the tongue allow for the pronunciation of certain letters, such as "k" and "g."

TONGUE

The front portion of the tongue moves food around the mouth during the chewing process and pushes food against the teeth for grinding. While the bottom of the tongue is smooth, the top of the tongue is covered by a layer of bumps or papillae that grip the food and help it move around the mouth. About 10,000 taste buds are located in the papillae and are sensitive to sweet, salt, bitter, and sour tastes. As a person ages, the taste buds lose their sensitivity to taste. Once the food is chewed up and mixed with saliva to break down the nutrients, the back muscles of the tongue start the food to move toward the esophagus, or "windpipe," to pass through to the stomach.

CIRCULATORY SYSTEM

The body needs blood to flow to all the extremities for healthy living, and the body moves about 5 liters of blood continuously through the circulatory system from the heart and lungs through the blood vessels. The pumping of the heart allows the blood to move around the body as needed in three distinct ways: through the pulmonary circulation or lungs, the coronary circulation or heart, and the systemic circulation or the whole system.

As hollow tubes, the blood vessels circulate the blood by either transporting good oxygen or removing used oxygen. The three types of blood vessels include arteries, capillaries, and veins where the arteries carry the blood to the body, the capillaries connect the arteries to the veins, and the veins carry the blood to the heart again. There are about 100,000 miles of blood vessels in an adult.

BLOOD VESSELS

Blood vessels carry blood throughout the body but also provide the means to determine the health of an individual through measuring both pulse and blood pressure. The pulse rate is checked by the feeling of an artery that is close to the skin as the contraction of the artery indicates the pace of the beating heart. Blood pressure is measured to show the amount of energy being expended by the heart to move the blood around the body. The two numbers for blood pressure reading are the systole phase or beat and the diastole phase or relax which are measured in millimeters. With each beat of the heart, a column of mercury rises and falls, and this action is measured in millimeters. Normal blood pressure ranges from about 110 over 60 to about 150 over 80.

PULMONARY CIRCULATION

Pulmonary circulation refers to the movement of the blood from the heart to the lungs and back and is one phase of the circulatory system. The veins return used blood by entering the right atrium through two large veins called vena cavae. The right atrium fills with the used blood, and the heart pushes the blood through a valve to the right ventricle which pushes the blood toward the lungs through the pulmonary artery. The lung capillaries exchange the good blood for the bad blood, and the good, oxygen-refreshed blood moves to the left atrium where it is then passed through to the left ventricle and exits through the aorta or main artery. From the main artery, the blood travels to the rest of the body. The passage from the artery to ventricle is through a one-way valve that does not allow blood to pass back through.

CORONARY CIRCULATION

The heart is the hardest working muscle of the body, beating all the time, and needs its own nourishment to keep working as hard as it does. The blood travels through the tissues of the heart to keep it enriched and thriving. Heart disease occurs if there is a lack of good, oxygen-refreshened blood and the tissues suffer from damage. The capillaries located in the heart react to the quality of the blood just as the other parts of the body do. If the blood is compromised, the heart suffers. If the blood were to flow backward from artery to ventricle, the gases associated with blood, such as oxygen and carbon dioxide, might mix. This mixture could introduce serious poisoning to the body, and any damage would start at the heart.

SYSTEMIC CIRCULATION

The systemic circulation provides oxygen-rich blood to the rest of the tissues of the body, and the blood vessels work together to transport the blood. From the aorta, the blood is forcefully contracted into smaller arteries where the smooth hollow tubes allow for quick blood flow. The outside of the artery is strong, which allows the power of the heart to keep the blood moving at its strong pace. The blood enters the capillaries, and the exchange of good blood and bad blood is made so the veins can return the bad blood to the heart to restart the process. The blood also passes through the kidneys during systemic circulation where the waste will be filtered, a process known as renal circulation. The blood moves through the small intestine as well for portal circulation, and the portal vein passes through the liver to filter sugars from the blood for storage.

HEART ATTACK

Most heart attacks occur at a slow pace with mild pain or vague discomfort. Signs of an impending heart attack include chest discomfort, upper body discomfort, shortness of breath, or lightheadedness. The pain in the chest may come and go but can feel like squeezing or fullness or just uncomfortable pressure. Discomfort could occur in other parts of the body, such as the arms, back, neck, or jaw. Shortness of breath may also accompany these feelings of pressure or pain, as well as the development of nausea or lightheadedness or breaking out in a cold sweat. Women are more likely than men to experience some of the symptoms other than chest pain, but the response to these symptoms should be less than 5 minutes to prevent death.

STROKE

The warning signs of a stroke can occur faster or more altogether than the warning signs of a heart attack and are just as terrifying. These warning signs include sudden numbness or weakness in the face, arm, or leg and usually on one side. A person could have confusion or trouble speaking or understanding. Sudden vision problems can also be exhibited. Any difficulty walking or maintaining balance and coordination with no reason and sudden massive headaches with no known explanation are also signs of possible stroke. The time of the symptoms should be verified as a clot-busting medicine can be administered within 3 hours of the start of the symptoms to reduce any long-term disability.

CHILDREN'S' HEART DISEASE

Heart disease in children occurs in two types: congenial and acquired. Congenital heart disease or congenital heart defect is in place at birth and cannot be contracted or passed on to other children. There are 35 known defects, and research is still ongoing. Some known defects include patent ductus arteriosis, atrial septal defects, and ventricular septal defects. Acquired heart disease occurs at some point during childhood and includes such diseases as rheumatic fever, infective endocarditis, and Kawasaki disease, which affects children five years old and younger. Each year sees about 40,000 children born with a defect, and most children can have these defects corrected through surgery. These defects could not have been prevented, and there are approximately 1 million Americans with cardiovascular defects.

NEURONS

The cell body contains the nucleus, ribosomes, endoplasmic reticulum, and mitochondria. The neuron can only survive if the cell body does. The axon is a cable-like projection of the cell body carrying the electrochemical signals the length of the cell. Axons can be covered with a thin layer of myelin, which is made of fat and speeds any signal of the nerve impulse along the axon. Myelinated neurons occur in the sensory and motor nerves while non-myelinated neurons occur in the brain and spinal cord. Dendrites, or nerve endings, connect cell bodies to each other and are small, branch-like projections of the cell.

SKIN

Skin is the largest organ of the human body and serves as protection for all internal organs, bones, and fluids. Skin has three layers: epidermis, dermis, and subcutaneous fat and allows the different systems of the human body to interact for the purpose of maintaining body temperature. The blood vessels, hair, and sweat glands work together by releasing sweat to cool off or causing blood to move closer to the surface of the skin to warm up. Most bodies operate at a normal temperature of 98.6 ° Fahrenheit (37° Celsius) to keep the body cells healthy. The hypothalamus works as the body's temperature gauge and controls the body's response to the temperature by sending signals to the skin to produce sweat or move blood.

EPIDERMIS

The epidermis is the top layer of skin visible on the whole body. The skin cells on the top of the skin are actually dead cells that are preparing to be sloughed off. The human body loses about 40,000 skin cells a day. Those dead cells protect the body and will give way to new cells that have been traveling to the top for more than 2 weeks. The body is always making new skin cells to replace old ones, and almost 95% of the cells in the epidermis work to make new ones. The other skin cells produce melanin, a substance that gives the body its color. Unprotected exposure to sun rays increases a person's chances for developing skin cancer.

DERMIS

The dermis is the layer of skin beneath the epidermis that contains nerve endings, oil glands, sweat glands, blood vessels, and the tough and stretchy proteins collagen and elastin. Nerve endings send signals to the brain about the condition of objects that come into contact. These nerve endings and muscles work together and will transmit signals to remove a hand from a hot surface instantaneously. Oil glands produce sebum, natural oil that keeps the skin lubricated and protected, and prevents water from being absorbed. Sweat glands produce a little sweat all the time, and the combination of the sweat and sebum forms a sticky substance that allows people to pick up objects. The blood vessels transport the oxygen and nutrients needed by the body and remove the waste.

SUBCUTANEOUS FAT

The subcutaneous fat is the bottom layer of skin that helps the body stay warm, provides shock protection during physical encounters, and holds the skin to the tissues beneath it. Hair starts at the subcutaneous fat level by growing out of a tube called a follicle. Each follicle grows through the layers of skin to the surface and also provides warmth for the body. Hair follicles exist over the entire body except for the lips, palms, and soles of feet, and there are over 100,000 hair follicles on the head. Some areas of the body have more hair follicles than others and the sebaceous glands that release the sebum in the skin provide the shine in hair and give it some waterproofing.

HAIR

Hair grows from the root at the subcutaneous fat, through the dermis and epidermis, and above the skin surface. The tiny blood vessels at the base of each follicle continue to feed the growing strand of hair, and the cells die once the hair passes the top layer of skin. All visible hair is dead cells, and an adult loses between 50 and 100 strands of hair each day. New hairs are always replacing fallen hairs, and each hair grows for about 5 years to survive for a few months before falling away. The cycle of hair growth is continuous. Uncut hair can grow up to 5 feet though most hairs grow at about 1/2 inch a month.

HAIR COLOR

As with the color of skin, the pigment melanin determines the color of hair. Darker colors such as black or brown have a higher concentration of melanin than do lighter colors such as blond or red. As people age, they lose the melanin pigment in their hair. This causes hair color to fade or turn gray or white. The color of hair is often related to the color of skin, so a light-skinned person may have light colored hair while a darker-skinned person may have darker hair. The hair follicles determine the structure of the hair, such as straight or curly, and the quality of the hair, such as coarse or fine.

HAIR CARE MAINTENANCE

Depending on the type of hair and the activities of the individual, hair should be cleaned routinely and frequently. A gentle shampoo and warm water is recommended for the most effective cleaning, and any lathering should be done with the fingertips and not nails. Conditioners can also be added to the regimen for untangling hair and making hair appear smooth, though the wrong kind of conditioner can make the hair appear oily or flat. Hair should be rinsed with lots of clean water and gently toweled dry. Wide-tooth combs instead of large brushes should be used to untangle hair. Shampoos and conditioners are usually formulated for a specific kind of hair, such as oily or normal. A healthy diet also produces healthier hair.

CELL TYPES

Cells make up every part of the human body and act as the basic functional and structural units of each system. While there are many different types of cells, such as nerve, hair, egg, sperm, muscle, and rod, in the human body, all life forms are made up of two basic cells: prokaryotic and eukaryotic. The prokaryotic cells have no nucleus and are the building blocks of bacteria. Eukaryotic cells have a nucleus and make up the human body. The human cell has a membrane, a nucleus, cytoplasm, organelles, and villi, as well as proteins and fat or lipids, and is composed mostly of water which makes it susceptible to interaction with other chemicals.

MEMBRANE

The human cell is enclosed within a membrane, or plasma membrane, and contains the nucleus and cytoplasm. Membranes are made up of 60% protein and 40% fat or lipid. The membranes function to keep the cytoplasm contained, provide a selective barrier, transport proteins, communicate through receptors, and recognize other cells. Lipids provide for the building blocks of the membrane and the hormones that enable the communication between cells. The proteins provide the enzymes that act as catalysts and often lower the amount of energy needed to expedite a reaction between cells. Membranes allow for cross movement by either the passive process of diffusion or osmosis or the active process of active transport or endocytosis and exocytosis.

CELL MOVEMENT

PASSIVE PROCESS

There are three methods of movement under the passive process: simple diffusion, osmosis, and facilitated diffusion. Simple diffusion refers to the movement of a substance from a highly concentrated area to a lowly concentrated area and is affected by temperature, the substance's molecular weight, the cross-sectional area to be covered, and the distance. Osmosis is the dispersal of water across a semipermeable membrane similar to the cell membrane from a concentrated area of low solute, or substance dissolved in another substance, to high solute. Facilitated diffusion describes the movement of a substance over a cell membrane from a lowly concentrated area to a highly concentrated area and requires membrane proteins, or "carriers." As a molecule binds to the membrane protein, the change in the protein allows another substance to pass through the membrane and into the cell.

ACTIVE PROCESS

The active process of cell movement is determined by the energy released by cells, and there are two different forms of the active process. Active transport refers to the movement of a substance from a lowly concentrated area to a highly concentrated area across the cell membrane facilitated by a carrier molecule while endocytosis and exocytosis refer to the movement of material in or out of the cell in bulk form. The membrane transport protein, or "carrier," prevents materials from entering the cell in its closed configuration until the transported substance binds to the carrier at the active or binding site. Once inside the cell, the transported material binds to another site on the carrier, which causes a change in the molecule that opens the cell membrane. Once the substance enters, the transported material separates from the carrier, and the opening is closed again.

ENERGY USAGE

The work done by cells consists of active transport, muscle contraction, synthesis, and impulse transmission and must be supported by energy. Cells capture and store energy and subsequently release energy as needed for the specific tasks required. Glucose supplies that energy. Cells break down glucose gradually in a series of chemical reactions and utilize the smaller amounts of energy from these reactions to produce Adenosine Triphosphate (ATP) that can also be broken down. This

energy released allows for the ability of the cell to perform the tasks necessary, such as contraction and synthesis and others. Since large amounts of ATP are needed, cells continue to perform the chemical breakdown of glucose and are assisted by the hydrogen transfer of oxidation that occurs in the mitochondria.

Hydrogen Transfer

Hydrogen transfer occurs in the mitochondria of the cell body. This type of oxidation describes how pairs of hydrogens transfer between substances and can create energy by moving between the substances. The hydrogens that are successfully transferred are called hydrogen carriers, and these hydrogen carriers release the energy required to make ATP. The hydrogens come from glycolysis, which involves the breakdown of glucose. While cells receive glucose from the blood, the blood glucose levels are maintained by the interaction of glycogen from the glucose produced in the liver and skeletal muscles after a meal, or glycogenesis, and the breakdown of that glycogen after the digestion, or glycogenolysis. This glucose breakdown produces the hydrogens that, in turn, allow the mitochondria to produce energy.

Nucleus

The nucleus is the blueprint for how people look and act by providing the genetic framework for all chemical reactions in the body. Acting as storage for the individual chemical components, or "genes," on the chromosomes, the nucleus also organizes these genes into the specific set of chromosomes to allow for cell division. The nucleus carries the regulatory factors and genetic components by way of the nuclear pores and produces messages that can code for proteins needed in various reactions as well as ribosomes in the nucleolus. Finally, the nucleus organizes the uncoiling of the DNA strands to replicate other genes. The nucleus is only 6 micrometers across, and each chromosome contains 1 long molecule of DNA.

Cytoplasm

As the watery fluid inside each cell, cytoplasm acts as the testing site for all metabolic reactions that might occur in the thickness of proteins, salts, sugars, carbohydrates, amino acids, nucleotides, and water. Cytoplasm has three main functions of energy, storage, and manufacturing. Animal cells contain more cytoplasm than plant cells due to the size of the animal and the complexity of the cell. All parts of the cell are contained within the cytoplasm but the nucleus. The cytoskeleton, or network of fibers of protein, gives the cytoplasm its shape and structure and is made up of three types of proteins: microtubles to guide the chromosomes during cell division, intermediate filaments to maintain the shape, and microfilaments to contract muscles and maintain cellular shape.

Mitochondria

Mitochondria are the main energy center in eukaryotes and have inner and outer membranes. Believed to be the result of some bacteria picked up by early man, mitochondria have their own DNA structures and ribosomes, and those ribosomes closely resemble the ribosomes of bacteria.

Organelles

Organelles refer to the different functioning parts, or "organs," of the cell such as the mitochondria, nucleus, and ribosomes. These small parts work together for the maintenance and growth of the cell and are often grouped together in discussion of cellular descriptions.

VILLI

Villus, or villus for singular, describes the many short and narrow finger-like growths of tissue located in some parts of the body. The small intestine has the most villi and uses these growths to capture passing particles and absorb the appropriate nutrients into the blood stream.

RIBOSOMES

As the sites for all protein synthesis, ribosomes help change RNA into protein. Hundreds of thousands of ribosomes are found throughout the cells as the presence of protein is so important for cellular functionality. Ribosomes have no membrane and float freely through the cytoplasm.

PROTEIN

Proteins are intricate molecules with 20 different amino acids that can be arranged in different orders to create a polypeptide of thousands of amino acids in length. The variety for protein distribution is enormous in scope, which allows proteins to function as specific enzymes to assist in the metabolism of a cell.

ENZYMES

Enzymes are biological proteins that perform the chemical reactions that take place in the cell.

AMINO ACIDS

Amino acids are found in proteins and assist in workings of the cell. There are 20 amino acids related to human proteins.

NERVOUS SYSTEM

The nervous system is made up of the brain, spinal cord, and neurons and includes the different types of nervous systems, such as peripheral, somatic, autonomic, and central. All nervous system tissue is made up neurons and glial cells. Neurons send and receive the messages for the body, and glial cells often surround the neurons and are in direct contact. The nervous system allows a body to maintain itself as well as monitor the environment by receiving sensory input, integrating that input, and responding to stimuli. Almost every organ and system in the body is controlled by the nervous system and provides constant feedback through different sensory transmissions. Larger animals with great mobility have the most developed nervous system of all living things.

NEURONS

As the functional unit of the nervous system, neurons number about 100 billion for the human brain and have three parts: dendrite, cell body, and axon. The dendrite receives information from other cells and passes that information to the cell body, which contains the nucleus and other organelles found in eukaryotic cells. The cell body transmits messages through the axon which conducts those messages on through the body. The three types of neurons include the sensory neurons, which usually have a long dendrite and short axon to carry messages from the sensory receptors to the central nervous system; motor neurons, which usually have a long axon and short dendrite to carry messages from the central nervous system to the muscles or glands; and the interneurons, which are found in the central nervous system only and connect neurons to each other.

A SYNAPSE

The meeting place between a nerve cell and any other cell is called a synapse. Information travels within the neuron as the electrical action potential, which is the change in condition of the negative

or positive charge of the membrane, and causes the polarity to adjust to this message. The space between the cells is the synaptic cleft, and neurotransmitters allow information to cross this space. These neurotransmitters are stored in synaptic vesicles, which are very small and located at the top of the axon, and can be either molecules or hormones. The time for the neurotransmitter to conduct information is between .5 and 1 millisecond, and neurotransmitters are then dissolved by specific enzymes in the synaptic cleft, pushed out of the cleft, or reabsorbed by the cell.

PERIPHERAL NERVOUS SYSTEM

The peripheral nervous system is made up of nerves only and allows the brain and spinal cord to connect to the rest of the body. The axons and dendrites of the neurons are encompassed by a white myelin sheath, the formation of axons wrapped together and formed from the plasma membranes of specialized glial cells. The cell bodies are located in the central nervous system or ganglia, which are collections of nerve cell bodies. The cranial nerves in the peripheral nervous system transmit messages back and forth between the brain and the body. Spinal nerves transmit messages back and forth between the spinal cord and the body. The two important parts of the peripheral nervous system are the sensory pathways between the body and the central nervous system and the motor pathways between the central nervous system and the muscles and glands.

SENSORY RECEPTORS

The peripheral nervous system handles most sensory information though this information is usually kept below the level of conscious recognition. The information that reaches the conscious level of recognition merely enhances a person's perception of the environment. The sensory receptors of the nervous system react to change in both the internal and external environment, such as pressure, hormone levels, taste, sound, or light, and convert this awareness into impulses that are sent to the brain or spinal cord. It is in the sensory centers of the brain and spinal cord that the information received is integrated and to which the body responds. This response as a motor output becomes a signal to the body parts or organs to convert the signal into an appropriate response or action, such as change in heart rate or simple movement.

SOMATIC NERVOUS SYSTEM

The somatic nervous system refers to all the nerves that control the muscular system and any corresponding external sensory receptors, like skin. Muscle fibers are effectors, as are gland cells and an automatic involuntary reaction to stimulus is the reflex arc. Any response to stimulus is involuntary, and the central nervous system does not control the response but is aware of the response. Such automatic involuntary responses include the knee jerk at the doctor's office, the need for maintaining balance, involuntary blinking, and involuntary stretching. The somatic nervous system enables the peripheral nervous system and the central nervous system to respond to sensory input and transmit that information to the appropriate body part or system.

AUTONOMIC NERVOUS SYSTEM

The autonomic nervous system can transmit inhibitory signals through the motor neurons whereas the somatic nervous system cannot. The autonomic nervous system consists of motor neurons that can control the internal organs, such as the heart muscle and smooth muscles in the intestine and bladder, and has two subsystems: the sympathetic nervous system and the parasympathetic nervous system. The sympathetic nervous system controls the involuntary fight or flight response while the parasympathetic nervous system controls relaxation. These two subsystems operate in the reverse of each other. Both systems can jump start an organ and then slow it down again: when a person experiences fear, the heart beats quicker; when a person calms down, the heartbeat slows down. The motor neurons in the autonomic nervous system connect to secondary motor neurons which cause the muscle reaction to outside stimuli.

CENTRAL NERVOUS SYSTEM

Composed of the brain and spinal cord, the central nervous system is surrounded by the bones of the skull and the vertebrae, as well as fluid and tissue. The brain is composed of three parts: cerebrum, cerebellum, and medulla oblongata. The cerebrum contains conscious awareness of the environment while the cerebellum and medulla oblongata contain subconscious awareness. The cerebrum controls intelligence and reasoning. The cerebellum is second largest and functions to coordinate muscles and maintain muscle tone. The medulla oblongata is closest of the three to the spinal cord and regulates the heartbeat and reflex centers for such reactions as coughing, sneezing, or hiccupping. The hypothalamus directs homeostasis, or the tendency of the body to maintain a certain temperature, as well as the feelings toward hunger and thirst and links up to the endocrine system while the thalamus acts as the center point for all incoming messages.

BRAIN

The brain begins as a tube in early development and then branches out to form the three parts of the brain (i.e., cerebrum, cerebellum, medulla oblongata) and the spinal cord. The brain stem is continuous with the top of the spinal cord. The medulla oblongata and corresponding pons control heart rate, digestion, blood vessel constriction, and respiration. The cerebellum is not considered part of the brain stem but functions to monitor balance and motor coordination. The cerebrum is divided into right and left hemispheres that are connected by the corpus callosum and covered by a thin layer of gray matter called the cerebral cortex, and the cerebrum is the part dedicated to intelligence, memory, and reasoning. The spinal cord links the brain to the rest of the body, carrying messages and initiating some reflexes that do not involve the brain.

CHEMISTRY

All objects are composed of three things basically: matter, energy, and empty space. The study of chemistry analyzes how those interact. Most living things are composed of the six elements carbon, hydrogen, nitrogen, oxygen, phosphorous, and sulphur. Other elements occur in nature but only in miniscule amounts. The most basic form of matter is an element, a substance that cannot be separated into parts by chemical methods. A combination of two or more elements is a compound. Elements are made up of atoms, which are identical particles defined as the smallest particle into which an element can be divided and still maintain properties of that element. A molecule is the joining together of two or more atoms by molecular bonds.

ATOM

Atoms are organized into protons, neutrons, and electrons. Protons are positively charged particles that weigh one atomic mass unit (amu). Neutrons have no charge and weigh one amu. Electrons are negatively charged and weigh 1/2000th of a proton or 0 amu. Particles that are similarly charged repel each other while particles with opposing charges, such as electrons and protons, attract each other. Protons and neutrons compose the nucleus or center of the atom while the electrons orbit the nucleus and are held in place by the attraction of opposing charges. The atomic number refers to the number of protons in the nucleus of an atom, and atoms with an equal number of protons to electrons are balanced and have no charge. The atomic mass refers to the number of protons and neutrons in the nucleus.

ENERGY IN ATOMS

Electrons orbit the nucleus in certain paths or orbitals. The closest energy level holds two electrons in one orbital, and the next energy level holds eight electrons in 4 orbitals with the next energy level holding eight electrons in 4 orbitals and so on. Energy levels containing the maximum number of electrons are considered filled and are inert or very stable. Most atoms with unfilled energy

levels react to fill the outer energy level and, in so doing, change to something else. Sodium has 1 electron in its outer level and is very unstable, and chlorine has 7 electrons in its outer level and is unstable. These two elements join together easily and often. As the number of electrons in the outer level increases, the atom becomes more stable. The electron has more potential energy the farthest it is from the nucleus.

MOLECULAR BONDS

When two or more atoms link together, they become molecules. There are three types of chemical bonds:

14. Covalent bonds are the most common and occur when a pair of electrons is shared by two or more atoms. A single bond occurs when only one electron is shared, and a double bond occurs when two electrons are shared
15. Hydrogen bonds occur between the negative pole of a polar molecule, or an unequally distributed number of orbiting electrons, and the slight positive charge on a hydrogen atom participating in another polar molecule. Water is a prime example with oxygen forming and reforming with hydrogen
16. Ionic bond occur when there is a total transfer of electrons from one molecule to another and is most common when a molecule needs just one or two electrons to fill the outer level. These bonds are not as strong as covalent and will fall apart in water

WATER'S CHEMICAL PROPERTIES

As a compound, water has many qualities that make it fundamental to chemistry. Living organisms are made up of between 50% and 90% water. Water is slow to heat up and to release heat since more heat is needed to raise the temperature of water than that needed by other liquids. This gives water the highest specific heat of all other liquid forms of compounds. Water also has a high heat of vaporization, which explains how sweating cools a body down. Water molecules tend to cling to each other and can exhibit a high surface tension. Water floats as ice and can dissolve most substances but with a tendency to dissociate into hydrogen ions and hydroxide ions.

ACIDS, BASES, AND PH

Acids are substances that release hydrogen ions (H+) which are always positive when dissolved in water whereas bases accept hydrogen ions, which increases the number of hydroxide ions (OH-) which are always negative. This concentration of hydrogen ions is fundamental to cells since many chemical processes only occur at the proper rate under specific hydrogen ion concentrations. These concentrations are measured by the pH scale which classifies all concentrations between 0 as the most acidic and highest hydrogen ion concentration to 14 as the most basic and lowest hydrogen ion concentration. Pure water is neutral and has a pH of 7. Life processes occur at the optimal speed at pH concentrations of a 6.5 to 7.5 range.

HAIR STRUCTURE

Hair is made up of very strong structural protein or keratin. This protein also makes up the nails and outer layer of the skin. Each strand of hair consists of three parts: the medulla, cortex, and cuticle. The medulla is the innermost layer and is only present in large, thick hairs. The cortex is the middle layer and provides strength as well as the color and texture of hair. The cuticle is the outermost layer and is thin and colorless. The cuticle protects the cortex. The hair root is enclosed inside a hair follicle and is below the surface of the skin. The dermal papilla is at the base of the hair root and is nourished by the bloodstream to produce new hair.

HAIR GROWTH CYCLE

There are three phases in the hair growth cycle constantly being repeated by hair follicles. The first phase is the Anagen or growth phase. This phase can range from 2 to 6 years with each hair growing 10cm a year but unlikely to grow more than a meter long. At any one time, the Anagen phase refers to 85% of all hairs. The Catagen or transitional phase describes the shrinkage of the hair follicle to about 1/6 of the normal length. This phase lasts between 1 and 2 weeks, and the lower part of the hair is destroyed with the dermal papilla breaking away from providing nourishment. The Telogen or resting phase refers to the 5 to 6 weeks where the hair does not grow but remains attached to the follicle. At any one time, the Telogen phase refers to between 10% and 15% of all hairs.

HAIR LOSS

The hair growth cycle repeats, and the dermal papilla joins again with the base of the follicle to restart the process. If the old hair has not been shed by brushing or some other force, the new hair pushes out the old one to facilitate the repeated process. The dermal papilla is important to hair growth since the receptors for male hormones and androgens are passes along through the bloodstream. Androgens can cause the hair follicle to progressively shrink and become finer which could lead to hair loss. Causes of hair loss are varied, and there are specific treatments for different types of loss. The six major types of hair loss include Alopecia Areata, Androgenetic Alopecia, Anagen Effluvium, self-induced hair loss, Telogen Effluvium, and scarring Alopecia.

Syphilitic Alopecia occurs as a manifestation or secondary syphilis where the hair loss is patchy and appears to be moth eaten. Penicillin is often used to treat this condition, and diagnosis is made through blood tests or microscopic examinations. Scleroderma causes fibrosis, or the hardening and tightening, of the skin as the result of excessive collagen production. This excess collagen interferes with the normal function of hair follicles and hair growth. This disease can affect small sections or areas of the head or body, but it can affect internal organs as well. The more severe case is called Systematic Scleroderma and affects women aged between 40 and 60 years. Tinea Capitis is highly contagious, also referred to as ringworm, and appears on the scalp. Scaling and redness occur in an area of stubbled hair loss where the Tinea digests the keratin of the hair and slowly expands. Shampoos and oral medication can correct this disease.

SELF-INDUCED HAIR LOSS

Self-inflected damage may result in the loss of hair. The two main types are Trichotillomania and Traction Alopecia. Trichotillomania results from continuous pulling of hair or plucking out strands and occurs most often in young children, adolescents, and women with twice as many women experiencing this type of hair loss as men. Distinct patches of hair are pulled from the scalp, but some sufferers also pull out the eyelashes or eyebrows. Treatment usually includes counseling or psychiatric assistance, and anti-depressants may be prescribed in severe cases. Traction Alopecia is the result of excessive pulling of hair due to different hairstyles, such as ponytails, braiding, and cornrows. This continued traction results in temporary hair loss. However, permanent damage may occur in excessive traction done over long periods of time. A change in the styling can greatly affect the Traction Alopecia.

ALOPECIA AREATA

Thought to be an auto-immune disease where the immune system attacks the follicles, Alopecia Areata appears at first as a rounded patch of bare skin about an inch in diameter. This disease affects men and women equally and usually starts in childhood. One person in 100 will experience Alopecia Areata at some point. While many people suffering from Alopecia Areata experience hair loss and then regrowth, about 20% of the cases experienced reoccurrences and then permanent loss. Three types of Alopecia Areata refer to the severity of hair loss: Alopecia Areata causes patches of loss on the scalp; Alopecia Totalis causes complete loss on the scalp; and Alopecia Universalis causes complete loss across the body. When the white blood cells called T-lymphocytes no longer attack hair follicles, hair is able to regrow.

TREATMENTS

There are treatments for sufferers of Alopecia Areata which are divided into groups based on the percentage of hair loss. For patients with less than 50% hair loss, treatments include cortocosteroids as a cream or lotion directly applied to the scalp or injections; dithranol as an ointment and also used in treatment for psoriasis; Retin-A Tretinoin as a gel and also used for acne; Topical Minoxidil which is marketed as Rogaine; and zinc.

For patients with more than 50% hair loss, the treatments include systematic cortisone as an oral medication or injections; PUVA as the oral medication psoralen combined with frequent treatments of UVA exposure for specified periods; irritants which cause an allergic reaction and draws the T-lymphocytes away from the follicles; and immuno-suppressive drugs similar to those used after organ transplant surgery.

There is no cure for Androgenetic Alopecia, but there are treatments. Minoxidil is marketed under Rogaine, gradually enlarging and lengthening hair follicles, and should be used for several months at a time and then continued. Propecia is a daily tablet for men only, preventing the shrinking of existing hair follicles, and should be taken for months at a time. Retin-A/Tretinoin as a gel should be applied at night and also treats acne. Zinc inhibits the production of dihodrotestosterone (DHT) which affects baldness and other diseases. Skinoren/Azelaic Acid is a new treatment for Androgenetic Alopecia but has been used to treat acne and is most effective at high concentrations. Saw Palmetto extract acts similarly to Propecia by lowering DHT but also blocks receptor sites on cell membranes that would absorb DHT, also treating diseases dependent on the production of DHT.

BASICS

Commonly referred to as male or female pattern baldness, Androgentic Alopecia accounts for 95% of hair loss in both men and women though more frequently in men. While women experience loss equally over the entire scalp, men experience loss with a receding hairline and then thinning hair on top. The enzyme testosterone converts the male hormone dihydrotestosterone (DHT) by the enzymes 5 alpha reductase which contributes to Androgenetic Alopecia in people who are genetically predisposed. People with a deficiency in 5 alpha reductase do not develop Androgenetic Alopecia because their bodies are unable to convert the testosterone into DHT. Large hair follicles shrink with each growth cycle, and the conversion of testosterone into DHT causes the hair shafts to produce smaller and finer hairs until nothing is left.

FEMALE PATTERN BALDNESS

There are treatments specifically for female pattern baldness. Diane 35 works as a hormonal contraceptive tablet to treat acne and excess facial hair or hirsutism and control Androgenetic Alopecia by blocking the male hormones and sometimes causing hair thickness to occur. Cimetidine is marketed as Tagamet and treats digestive disorders, the secretion of stomach acid, and hirsutism and blocks dihydrotstosterone (DHT). Cyproterone Acetate blocks the production of DHT and treats hirsutism in women and reduces sexual aggression in men. Spironolactone works similarly to Cimetidine by preventing DHT but also treats blood pressure. Nizoral/Ketoconazole reduces testosterone production and treats fungal infections on the scalp and can be used as a shampoo formula in combination with treatments of Androgenetic Alopecia.

ANAGEN EFFLUVIUM

Anagen Effluvium causes sudden hair loss in response to chemicals or radiation similar to chemotherapy. The hair never enters the resting stage but is suddenly lost in a 1- to 3-week period after exposure. Exposure to toxic chemicals like Thallium and Arsenic also produce this type of sudden hair loss. Hair could come out in clumps or whole sections disappear in days. Anagen Effluvium occurring as a result of chemotherapy is temporary as hair growth returns to normal after treatment in most cases. Some sufferers have experienced fuller growth once the exposure was removed. The texture can be different with the regrown hair. Most patients who anticipate the chemotherapy may cut their hair very short or shave their heads bald to accommodate a wig during therapy.

TELOGEN EFFLUVIUM

Telogen Effluvium occurs during sudden stress where hair follicles stop growing and enter the resting phase for 3 months before a large amount of hair is shed. The stress usually has abated by that time, but the loss may continue until the stress-causing issue is corrected. More women than men experience Telogen Effluvium. After childbirth, women will lose hair because of the hormonal shift taking place in the body but notice the correction within 9 months. Abortions or miscarriages can also cause hair loss due to the sudden change in hormones. Taking a birth control pill can cause hair loss and thinning due to the presence of testosterone, and certain prescribed medications may also cause hair loss. Surgery or emotional stress can also result in hair loss. Hair loss as the result of thyroid gland malfunction, diabetes, anemia, or Systemic Lupus Erythematosis will continue until the cause is treated.

SCARRING ALOPECIA

Scarring Alopecia occurs when follicles become infected, and rough patches occur on the scalp. Scarring Alopecia caused by Discoid Lupus Erythematosus is shown by lesions that eventually become smooth atrophic and scarred. Topical corocosteroid ointments provide the most help for small lesions. An inflammatory disease that usually strikes skin and mucous membranes, Lichen Planus starts as an itchy patch on the wrists and forearms and can appear on the scalp as raised reddish-purple areas. Steroid lotions can relieve the itchiness, while antimalarial drugs can reduce the inflammation. Pseudopelade of Brocq is a rare Scarring Alopecia with no potential for regrowth and usually affects middle-aged people. Aplasia Cutis Congenita is also rare but results in small blisters usually in the midline of the scalp, appearing at birth and fading away. Congenital Atrichia occurs at birth and usually fades as hair follicles form in certain areas.

HAIR ANALYSIS

Different chemicals, toxins, and radiation are present in the body and embedded in the protein in hair. A three-inch strand of hair can attest to the condition of the body for a 6-month period. Specific elements, usually toxic, are associated with pathological disorders. The levels of these elements in hair provide an excellent tool for analysis that is much cleaner than blood or urine and preferred for drug testing and forensic analyses. A hair analysis can identify an illness and its source, and the interpretation of the analysis is the most important part for recovery. There are roughly 70,000 chemicals exposing each day and 14,000 chemicals in the foods commonly eaten. By analyzing the chemical toxins, vitamins, and minerals in hair, scientists can better recommend improvements to prevent possible disorders or disease.

PROTECTING HAIR

Hair can be damaged in many ways. Here are suggestions for protecting hair. The chlorine in swimming pools can discolor hair and give it a sickly tinge because of the strong bleach. Before

38

swimming, people should apply a deep conditioner. Afterward, swimmers can rinse with apple cider vinegar and then club soda to lift out excess salt and chlorine. Sunscreen or a mixture of 1/2 cup water and 1/2 teaspoon of 25 SPF sunscreen can be applied to hair for sun protection, or a lip balm of a high SPF factor can be used on sections. The best way to sun-proof the color is to use a darker shade of blond or brunette to anticipate fading or to use a color-locking gloss treatment for reds. The blow dryer should be set on a temperature that does not make your head uncomfortably warm.

FINGERNAILS

Fingernails protect fingers, improve a person's dexterity, and can reveal information about a person's health. Though nail growth begins at the matrix, the physical condition of the nails can appear flat, ridged, smooth, dented, or unusually colored and can be improved through proper care or even medication. Nails are the laminated layers of keratin, a kind of protein also found in hair and skin. Each nail has five parts. The nail plate is the hard portion visible at the end of the finger. The nail folds frame the nail on three sides, and the nail bed is the skin beneath the nail plate. The cuticle is the tissue that overlaps the nail plate and protects new keratin cells that emerge from the nail bed. The lunula is half-moon shape at the base of the nail that appears whitish.

NAILS AND HEALTH

Fingernails show a great deal about a person's health and can indicate if there is a health issue that needs to be corrected. The harmless conditions of nails include vertical ridges, white lines, or spots, all issue that may become more visible with age. The white spots within the nail usually result from some kind of injury to the nail plate or nail bed and will grow out in time. Any yellow or green discoloration in the nails may be the result of a respiratory condition such as chronic bronchitis or lymphedema or swelling of hands. Severe illnesses may cause indentations across the nails from where the cuticle has been interrupted. Any persistent nail problem should be reported to a doctor who may examine the nails and other body parts to determine the proper diagnosis.

NAIL CARE MAINTENANCE

Simple guidelines can make the most of any nail care product or service. Fingernails should not be used as tools to pick things apart or poke through things. Any habits of biting the nails or cuticles should be stopped as this allows bacteria or fungi to enter any minor cut and cause paronychia, a nail infection. Injured nails show signs of damage for months due to the slow growth of nails. Gloves should be worn during soap and water cleaning or any work with harsh chemicals for long periods. Routine nail maintenance such as trimming and cleaning should be completed regularly, and any hangnails should be clipped off and not ripped out as the ripping pulls at the living tissue. Nails should be moisturized regularly as they require moisture just as the body does and especially after hand washing.

WEAK NAILS

Nails can be made tougher with several easy steps. Cuticles should never be removed from the finger as this leads to nail infection. Each manicurist should properly sterilize all tools used during the manicure process to prevent any spreading of viral infections such as Hepatitis B or warts. Weak or brittle nails should be kept short and square-shaped with slightly rounded tops and trimmed and moisturized after bathing. Hands should be moisturized and covered with cotton gloves during the night, and nail hardeners that do not contain toluene sulfonamide or formaldehyde could be applied. Any nail polish removers that use acetone should be avoided as it dries nails out, and nail polish removers should not be used more than twice a month. Split nails or torn nails can be repaired with nail glue or clear polish until the damage grows out or grows long enough to be cut.

FUNGAL NAIL INFECTION

An infection on the fingernail or toenail is caused by a fungus called onychomycosis and is more likely to occur on toenails than fingernails. This infection makes the nails thick and discolored or brittle and oddly shaped. Pain may even occur as the result of an infection. Fungal nail infections are more common in adults over 60 years and are especially common in people with circulation problems or diabetes. While anyone can contract a fungus nail infection, children hardly ever develop this kind of condition. Warm, wet places are perfect breeding grounds for a fungus to grow, and any kind of heavy boots or sweaty socks encourage fungus. Locker room floors and public showers are also good places for fungi to be picked up as are wet areas like dishwashers. Fungal infections can also be passed along through wet towels or washcloths.

DANDRUFF

The entire body continuously sheds dead skin cells, and the skin always sheds cells. These excess cells represent the skin cells being shed in the normal growing process of the skin cells located on the scalp. When this process becomes excessive, dandruff occurs but is the result of the natural growing process that involves living skin cells in addition to the dead cells that would normally be sloughed off. The two causes for dandruff are internal and external. Internal causes include hormonal changes, poor health and hygiene, lack of rest, hypersensitivity to allergens, excessive amounts of sugar or starch in the diet, emotional stresses, and a hereditary predisposition. External causes include an excessive us of styling products like hair spray, improperly used hair-coloring products, excessive use of hot hair curlers or irons, cold weather and dry heating, anxiety and stress, infrequent shampooing, and inadequate rinsing of the scalp and hair.

FUNGUS

While bacteria may aggravate the dandruff problem, bacteria do not cause the condition to occur initially. In its mildest forms, dandruff is considered to be a scalp or skin disease, and some have described it as seborrhea capitos or excessive sebum production of the scalp. Dandruff is associated with a small fungus called Pityrosporum ovale, or P. ovale, which lives on human bodies all the time and only becomes an issue when dandruff occurs. Known as "dry scalp," dandruff is a seasonal occurrence in most cases, popping up during the winter and appearing as small, whitish-gray patches or scaling. Oily scalps experience dandruff the most because of the propensity to support the growth of P. ovale. Dandruff cannot be cured but treated with shampoos and other products.

TREATING DANDRUFF

There are several shampoos on the market that specialize in dandruff treatment. Any use of a dandruff treating shampoo should be continued so that the condition does not reoccur. If the product does not work, the dandruff sufferer should consider trying another product. The scalp generates new batches of flakes every three days, and the use of a dandruff shampoo accompanied by a thorough cleansing of the scalp and hair will keep dandruff flakes from appearing for about three days. Mild shampoos such as Neutrogena, Head & Shoulders, and Selsun Blue should be used to control and prevent dandruff as most detergent-based shampoos can cause drying, which will only exacerbate the dandruff condition.

SEVERE DANDRUFF

For severe cases of dandruff, a dermatologist can prescribe special lotions or ointments for use to treat the problem. Ordinary products that contain zinc, pyritheone, or selenium sulfide most effectively rid the scalp of dandruff flakes. However, if the use of any of these products results in the scalp swelling, scabbing, or showing signs of redness or gooeyness in addition to the flakes, another scalp disease could be present, such as psoriasis or ringworm. A doctor should be consulted if any of these conditions exist. The only shampoo containing ketoconazole, Nizoral has been able to inhibit the growth of P. ovale, the fungus causing dandruff, as well as normalizing the pH of the scalp and has long-lasting effects. Nizoral continues to work several days after being rinsed, making it possible for sufferers to use this shampoo periodically without worry of reoccurrences.

DIET

Health and nutrition also play a part in the controlling of dandruff. Inefficient carbohydrates and fatty-acid metabolization can cause dandruff, so the diet should consist of foods that do not meet these criteria and have plenty of vitamin B, which can be found in nutritional yeast and raw wheat germ. A healthy diet to prevent dandruff should include eggs and cabbage as they provide vitamin B6 and sulphur, which a natural mineral for beautifying the scalp. While an allergy to dairy products such as milk or yogurt may cause dandruff, there are alternative food sources to provide vitamin B6 that should not have the dandruff side effects. Some bodies have a sensitivity to the allergens in chocolate, nuts, and shellfish, and this reaction could cause dandruff. Nuts and flax seed have good fats that benefit the body and support more healthy scalps, as well as garlic and oil of oregano.

PREVENTING DANDRUFF

Increasing the blood circulation of the head will also cut down on the production of dandruff. Using hot and then cold water on the head will increase circulation, and yoga headstands also help with the increased flow of blood. Outdoor exercise in the fresh air increases the circulation to the scalp, and careful brushing to loosen dead skin cells prior to shampooing hair also enervates the blood flow. If daily hair washing is part of the hair care routine, then small amounts of baby shampoo can be used. The harsh shampoos cause the sebaceous gland to produce more oil, which initiates the dandruff process. Rubbing a fresh onion over the scalp or washing with a sulphur-based shampoo will invigorate the hair and scalp. Hair dryers frequently dry out the scalp and should be avoided in the treatment of dandruff.

ROOT

The root is located beneath the skin where cells group together to form keratin, the protein needed to create hair. The root forms inside a follicle, is protected by the inner root sheath and outer root sheath, and grows through the skin. The Epithelial cells divide around the papilla and form the hair shaft and hair sheath.

BULB

The bulb is located at the base of the hair follicle and includes the root which surrounds the hair papilla.

PAPILLA

The papilla is located at the center base of the hair bulb and nourishes the root as it is held in the center of the follicle.

SHAFT

The shaft is the inner three layers of the hair root and around the papilla. These three layers form the medulla or innermost core, the cortex or highly keratinized bulk, and the cuticle or hard outer layer.

BODY HAIR

All hair is made of keratin, the same hard protein found in fingernails and toenails, and grows from the root and through the skin.

VELLUS HAIR

Vellus hair is the soft, fine, short hair usually on women's backs chests, and faces. This hair usually adopts the same color as the skin and helps maintain the body temperature by providing some form of insulation.

TERMINAL HAIR

Terminal hair is darker, coarser, and thicker than vellus hair and usually grows on the head. At puberty, terminal hair grows in the armpits and pubic regions. For men, terminal hair also grows on the face, chest, legs, and back and provides both cushioning and protection.

HIRSUTISM

Hirsutism is excessive hair growth and can result from certain medical conditions or response to medication such as anabolic steroids. Women may experience polycystic ovary syndrome which causes dark coarse hairs to appear on the upper lip, arms, chest, and legs.

SCABIES

Though common in children under 2 years, scabies is also endemic to tropical areas and is caused by Sarcoptes scabiei mite infestation. The female mite burrows into the skin to lay 10 to 25 eggs and then dies. The eggs hatch within 3 or 4 days and mature within 14 to 17 days. Prolonged skin contact allows the female mite to transfer, and common places are at hospitals or nursing homes and daycares, wherever there is regular household contact such as shared clothing or bedding. Symptoms include severe itching which may last for 1 month after treatment.

BLISTERS

Blisters can be small or large fluid-filled lesions that may result from insects, pets, medication, friction, burns, or other systemic causes such as diabetes or lupus. Blisters may dissolve on their own or can be treated by a doctor.

ACNE

Acne is a common skin disorder affecting 17 million people across the country and at all ages. While acne can occur on the face, arms, back, and neck, acne begins as a clogged pore where oil cannot escape. This breeding area for bacteria can result in blackheads or pus-filled cysts which could leave scars. Hormones, especially testosterone, trigger acne outbreaks and are at the most sensitive point during adolescent to teenage years and especially for young boys. It was believed erroneously that certain foods or even stress cause acne outbreaks, but only such factors as constrictive helmets or collars, pollution, hormonal changes, harsh facial scrubbing, or picking at the skin can exacerbate the skin disorder. Acne is often treated by medication or certain facial creams.

RINGWORM

A fungal infection of the skin, ringworm is a rash that is ring- or oval-shaped and can occur anywhere on the skin and even in the hairline. Ringworm can attack the scalp and leave temporary bald sections of hair. This infection has nothing to do with worms but is the result of a fungus that spreads easily. In fact, ringworm is contagious from person to person through direct physical contact or secondary contact as with an article of clothing, such as a hat or jacket, or even specific hygienic items, such as a hairbrush or razor. People can even catch ringworm from household pets. Certain medications placed directly on the infected skin can cure ringworm, but more serious cases may require prescribed medication from a doctor

WARTS

Caused by the human papilloma virus (HPV), warts are highly contagious skin viruses that are easily spread among people. The common wart is a rough-looking lesion usually found on a person's hands or fingers. Smaller and smoother warts have also been known to develop on a person's hand or even face. Plantar warts occur on the soles of the feet and can be quite large in comparison to other warts, as big as a quarter. Warts located in the genital and anal areas are called genital warts and have increased in number and always require medical attention and treatment. Though warts are viruses, they occur spontaneously and sometimes disappear the same way. Some warts are reoccurring with no satisfactory scientific explanation, and researchers are continually searching for ways to cure them.

CURING WARTS

Verify that the growth is a wart and not just a skin rash by checking the surface (broken skin with tiny red dots) without touching directly or touching anyone else afterwards. Always wash with warm water when dealing with warts. Adhesive tape applied directly to the wart has proven more effective than creams. The acid in castor oil irritates the wart, and vitamin C paste is also acidic enough to irritate. Hot water has been known to soften plantar warts, and over-the-counter remedies have the best success for overnight use. Some doctors have noticed success with powers of suggestion on smaller children by putting chalk over the infected area, and most doctors believe that footwear and avoiding moist environments is usually sufficient protection. Warts will develop near scratches, so any open cut should be addressed immediately.

SHAMPOO

As a kind of creamy lotion that lathers, shampoo is used to cleanse the hair and scalp by removing dirt and grime without removing too many natural oils produced to maintain the scalp. Shampoos contain cleansing as well as conditioning agents to coat the shaft to give the hair the appearance of shine and thickness. The conditioning portion smooths out the cuticle scales to prevent tangles and to help remove static from the strands of hair during and following the towel or forced-heat drying. Shampoos labeled "pH Balanced" possess the same acidity levels as the specific types of hair listed. Any person with damaged or chemically treated hair should choose these types of shampoos for the best cleansing possible. Healthy hair in good condition does not require the pH balanced shampoo if maintained by shampoo and conditioner.

The shampoo should be chosen based on the type of hair being cleaned, such as dry, normal, oily, or treated. The hair should be brushed first to untangle any knots and loosen any dirt or dead skin cells. The water should be kept at a lukewarm temperature to remove oily residues. Once the hair is wet, a small amount of shampoo should be worked throughout the hair and massaged onto the scalp with the fingertips with special focus on such areas as the hairline. Hair should be rinsed until the water is clear and repeated as necessary. Hair should be blotted with a clean towel to remove any excess water before conditioner is applied. Mild formula shampoos should be used and changed periodically to prevent the body from becoming resistant to the particular ingredients in the shampoo.

HAIR CONDITIONERS

Shampoo is often not enough to maintain healthy hair, so using a conditioner can enhance the shine or texture of the hair in addition to the ingredients used in regular shampoo. The cuticle scales of hair lie over each other in patterns to reflect light, a process that gives hair its shiny or glossy appearance. Styling, coloring, and relaxing all contribute to the breakdown of healthy hair by causing cuticles to lift and allowing moisture to be released from the cortex of the hair, which makes hair become dry while losing luster and tangling easier. Severely damaged cuticles can break

43

off and cause hair to become thin. Conditioners coat hair with a fine film that smooths the cuticle and enhances the glossiness of hair and should be left in for 3 to 5 minutes before being thoroughly rinsed out. Basic conditioners can be used every day.

HOT OILS

Hot oils, however, should be used weekly to deeply nourish and treat hair. Once heated, the hot oil should be massaged evenly onto the scalp and throughout the hair and left for 3 to 5 minutes. A shower cap can cover the head for a few extra minutes for more intensive treatment. Hair should be rinsed thoroughly and with a mild conditioning shampoo to prevent any appearance of greasiness.

INTENSIVE

Intensive conditioners are used weekly to help hair maintain the proper moisture balance and are recommended for damaged hair with split ends or dry and frizzy hair. The conditioner should be distributed evenly throughout the hair with special focus on the ends and left in for 3 to 5 minutes. Rinsing should be done with lots of water, and the hair should be lifted from the scalp to verify all conditioner is removed.

Three additional types of conditioners are also available for hair care maintenance.

LEAVE-IN

Leave-in treatments are designed to increase shine, retain natural moisture, and reduce static and can be used daily after shampooing and without rinsing out. Leave-in conditioners are especially good for fine or limp hair since they reduce hair care product overload on the weaker hair. These treatments are easy to use and can provide additional protection from heat styling.

PROTEIN RESTRUCTURERS

Protein restructurers are intensive protein conditioners that penetrate the cortex and help to repair and strengthen damaged hair. This treatment is especially good for hair that has lost its natural elasticity or flexibility from heat damage or chemical processing.

COLOR/PERM

Color/perm conditioners nourish and invigorate chemically treated hair and can form a protective layer around the porous areas of the hair to prevent any fading or any permanent relaxing.

SKIN TYPES

The best products for hair and skin are worthless if the correct type has not been selected. Different kinds of skin type include the following: oily, dry, normal, combination, and sensitive. Oily skin has large pores and a tendency towards blemishes caused by the production of sebum. Dry skin can often feel tight and uncomfortable as though being stretched, a feeling caused by too little oil in lower levels of skin and not enough moisture on the surface. Normal skin has a perfect balance of being smooth and evenly toned with no enlarged pores and few blemishes or dry patches. Combination skin may have sections of oily and dry skin with the central part or T-zone being one way and the cheeks another. Sensitive skin is finely textured and easily irritated.

OILY SKIN

Oily skin tends to show wrinkles less than other types due to the oil. Harsh products should not be used since oily skin is often sensitive and can become aggravated by mistreatment. The best products for oily skin gently remove oil from the surface and unclog pores without drying out skin. A foaming facial wash is best as it removes excess oil and dirt without stripping the skin of natural oils. An alcohol free astringent, or lotion causing tissue to contract, should be applied to remove any

44

oily residue and help tighten pores. A light moisturizer should be also be used to seal in water and keep skin hydrated properly and then blotted to absorb any excess oils prior to any further application of substances such as make-up or sunscreen.

DRY SKIN

Dry skin may feel tight and itchy with occasional flakes or peeling. This condition can be worsened by the use of soap or harsh toners, so soothing care should be taken to make the surface smooth and the skin nourished to its optimum moisture level. Cleansing should be done with a rich, creamy lotion to create emulsion, or even distribution of liquid particles to lift dirt and make-up from the surface of skin, and then carefully removed with a cotton pad. The face should be splashed with cool water to remove any excess cleanser and to refresh the skin. A rich creamy moisturizer with sunscreen to hold in moisture should be used to moisturize the upper levels of the skin and left on for a few minutes before any further application of substances such as make-up or sunscreen.

NORMAL SKIN

Normal skin type is considered quite rare and is highly envied by other people with differing skin types. Regardless of its perfect natural state, special care should be taken to maintain the health of the normal skin and not disturb its natural balance. The cleansing should be done with a gentle cleanser and massaged into the face for 30 second prior to any rinsing. The skin can be cooled with a refreshening toner and then smoothed with a moisturizing lotion that will naturally complement the balance of moisture and oil and maintain the quality of skin. Once this is completed, any additional substances such as make-up or sunscreen can be applied.

COMBINATION SKIN

Combination skin is comprised of dry and oily patches and so a dual process of skincare should be considered. The different areas of the skin should be handled separately as what works for one skin type will not work for the other, but the results will show softer and smoother skin that appears radiant. A foaming face wash should be used with special concentration on the oily areas to prevent clogged pores and possible blemishes. A creamy cleanser should be used in the evenings with special concentration on the dry areas to verify that they are soothed and cleaned daily. Moisturizer should be applied over the entire face with special concentration on the drier sections and then any excess blotted off from the oily sections with a clean tissue before any further application of substances such as make-up or sunscreen.

SENSITIVE SKIN

Sensitive skin is more likely to show redness and allergies and may be accompanied by broken veins across the cheeks and nose. This skin type requires incredibly gentle products which should be chosen from the hypoallergenic, or unlikely to cause a reaction, types specially formulated for sensitive skin. If any use of these types of products causes irritation, the areas affected should be cleansed with whole milk and moisturized with a solution or tincture, mixture of dissolved parts, of glycerin and rose water. Facial washes and soaps should be avoided as they will likely strip the skin of oils and moisture and thereby increase sensitivity. Warm water can be splashed on the face to remove any traces of the cleanser, and moisturizers that are unscented can be used to strengthen the skin and provide a barrier against various irritants. Additional substances such as make-up or sunscreen may then be applied.

MASSAGE

Massage is a physical stimulation for the increase and improvement of blood flow through the body that speeds up the release of metabolic waste from muscles. As a hand-on manipulation of the muscles, connective tissue, tendons, ligaments, and joints as well as other tissues of the body, massage therapy is an alternative health choice to reduce pain and the results of stress from everyday worries and work, pulled muscles, and other chronic pain syndromes. If used early enough after traumatic accidents or experiences, massage can greatly reduce the creation of painful muscular patterns. A massage therapist skillfully manipulates the soft tissue of a person as a way to relax and reduce stress or to relieve pain and prepare for sporting events.

BENEFITS

There are many benefits of massage therapy. Besides allowing a person to relax, massage can reduce tension in muscles and other kinds of discomfort endured by the body. Anxiety can also be lessened with massage, and sleep can be improved. A feeling of well-being is increased in the patient, as well as an improvement in the range of motion in muscles and joints. Tight muscles are relaxed with muscle aches and other stiffness being relieved. Massage allows for a speedy recovery after physical exercise or work and promotes healthy skin that is well-nourished as a result of the increase in blood flow. Massage also improves the functioning of the immune system and an overall sense of energy.

CRANIOSACRAL MASSAGE THERAPY

Craniosacral massage therapy is a noninvasive technique that encourages the improvement of the functions of the brain and spine to remove stress, promote good health, and resist disease by using the natural mechanisms of the body.

DEEP TISSUE MASSAGE

Deep tissue massage releases chronic muscle tension by using slower strokes with more direct pressure applied across the muscles. By identifying the stiff or painful areas through the noted quality of deep layer musculature, specific hand positions and strokes can slowly work release into the deeper layers of muscle tissue.

ESALEN MASSAGE

Esalen massage is a more philosophical approach improved upon Swedish massage and influenced by Esalen leaders Charlotte Selver and Bernie Gunther. This type of massage allows the therapist to meditatively provide needed services for the client and be aware of any changes in the client's needs.

SHIATSU

Shiatsu is a Japanese physical therapy for healing that helps many conditions such as poor health, menstrual pain, headaches, and injuries. As a deeply relaxing therapy, Shiatsu helps prevent the build up of daily stress. Focusing on the vital energy flowing through the body in a network of channels, or meridians, Shiatsu considers the person's health, the symptoms experienced, and the person's constitution and level of energy to improve the person's energy flow and is therapy for the whole being. With gentle holding, palm pressing, and pressure applied with thumbs, elbows, knees, and feet, Shiatsu improves the energy flow and affects the mental and emotional status of the person.

SWEDISH MASSAGE

This type of massage does not refer to the country of Sweden but to the techniques used that relax muscles with the application of pressure to deeper bones and muscles, which are rubbed in the same direction as the flow of blood returning to the heart. Veins and the lymph system carry blood back to the heart and are dependent on the muscle action more than the blood pressure to operate effectively. The friction associated with this massage is reduced by the use of oil or powder, and some massage therapists believe that vegetable rather than mineral oil is better. Swedish massage

relaxes muscles, increases circulation without affecting the heart's work, removes metabolic waste, shortens recovery time from strain, stretches ligaments and tendons, stimulates the skin and nervous system, and gives the person a sense of awareness of their body and its connectedness.

PFRIMMER DEEP MUSCLE THERAPY

Pfrimmer deep muscle therapy works across muscles that manipulate deep tissues, which stimulates circulation, improves lymphatic flow, and promotes health in stagnant tissues. This therapy was developed by Theresa Pfrimmer after partial paralysis and eventual recovery through this therapy.

NEUROMUSCULAR THERAPY

Neuromuscular therapy, such as the St. John Method, involves more advanced study in pressure therapy that breaks the tension-pain cycle by relaxing muscles to increase circulation and, thus, correct the body's neuromuscular integrity.

JIN SHIN DO

Jin Shin Do is a derivative of acupressure where gentle fingertip pressure is applied to 30 specific points on the body to release and balance energy. This therapy releases muscle tension, improves circulation, balances emotional levels, and enhances the spiritual self.

HAKOMI

Hakomi is a kind of psychotherapy that incorporates certain states of consciousness to probe the nonverbal levels of beliefs and experiences. This body-mind awareness combines with physical connections to allow the person to improve attitude.

TRAGER

Trager psychophysical integration incorporates light, nonintrusive movements to help release deep-seated body and thought patterns. Called Trager, this therapy moves each part of the body rhythmically to produce the feeling free and effortless movement which reduces stress from tension, teaches better stress recovery, enhances conscious awareness, improves self-image, and reduces rigidity. This form of therapy encourages a feeling of peace and serenity as an energy level beyond relaxation.

MYOFASCIAL

Myofascial evaluates and treats bodily restrictions in the contractile connective tissues or muscles and the noncontractile connective tissues or fascia through applying traction, pressure, and positioning. The fascia is a complicated network surrounding groups of muscle fibers and organs and supporting the body while affecting the musculoskeletal, nervous, and visceral or organ systems. Tense muscles can restrict the blood flow and affect the energy of the body, as well as shorten from improper use. Myofascial therapy relaxes muscles and loosens up fascia.

TRIGGER POINT & MYOTHERAPY

Trigger Point and Myotherapy refer to techniques that relieve pain and alleviate muscle cramps and spasms by locating and deactivating the trigger points or tender areas of muscle damage or painful muscle kinks. This therapy reduces muscle spasm, a condition maintained by the nervous system, by improving the blood flow into the trigger point area or ischemia. Pressure is applied to these points for 7 to 10 seconds of momentary pain but resulting relief. Ice or other cooling substances can reduce the nervous system response to pain. The muscles are then gently stretched to finish the relaxation. Myotherapy eases pain and soothes tight muscles and is best for people with chronic muscle tension.

POLARITY

Polarity therapy is a holistic belief that the energy fields should be balanced within the body to maintain proper physical and mental health. The energy flow is restricted by stress, tension, pain, and other outside stimuli, which are all issues that can keep a person from good health and spirituality. The energy blocks can be released through bodywork, exercise, diet, and self-awareness through gentle manipulation, holding pressure points or poles, counseling on positive thinking, diet combinations, and simple exercises to encourage positive energy flow. Founded by Dr. Randolph Stone DO, DC, ND, polarity therapy examines the interdependence of the body, mind, spirit, and emotions and is usually included with other therapies used to restore peace and improve the body.

ON-SITE OR CHAIR

Popular for office use as a benefit for employees or conference and workshop attendees, on-site or chair massage is a 15 to 20 minute session in a special chair where the person remains fully clothed. No oils are used, and the session relaxes the shoulders, neck, upper back, head, and arms.

REIKI

Reiki treatment involves a traditional patterned hand positioning on the body without using pressure to increase energy and to provide deep relaxation and healing. This occurs through channeling of the universal life-force energy

MANUAL LYMPHATIC DRAINAGE

The most popular form of massage, manual lymphatic drainage combines soothing, gentle massage-like movements in rhythmic and precise places to increase the flow of the lymphatic fluid throughout the body.

ROLFING

Rolfing aligns the major segments of the body through a deep manipulation or pressure on the fasica and other connective tissues.

SPORTS MASSAGE

Sports massage is used on athletes in training and focuses on the muscles that are used in the specific activity. By incorporating pre-event, post-event, and maintenance practices, sports massage promotes athletic endurance, greater performance, fewer chances for injury, and shorter time for recovery.

WATSU

Watsu is the combination of Shiatsu massage therapy and water treatments where the water allows for freer movements not possible on the massage table. The therapist floats the person in a warm pool cushioning the neck and supporting the back, and the person is swayed and stretched from side to side. The process is completed in quiet which allows the person's mind and body to relax.

THAI MASSAGE

The traditional massage of Thailand, Thai massage or Nuad Bo-Rarn involves pressure on the energy lines and points combined with stretching movements that affect the whole body's flexibility and release the body tensions while increasing energy flow.

SCALP TREATMENT

Maintaining the health of the hair and scalp is the main purpose of scalp treatment. Different types of hair and diseases or conditions of the scalp require different procedures to eradicate and repair the damage done to the scalp and subsequently to the hair. The different brand names and generic at-home remedies advise that not all treatments work for a particular person or on a particular condition, and there are many different types of scalp treatments available for the differing conditions. A doctor or dermatologist could be contacted if the traditional at-home remedies or drugstore purchases do not improve the condition of the scalp or if they make the condition worse. If any at-home remedy worsens the condition, then all use should be stopped and a doctor notified immediately.

RINGWORM SCALP TREATMENT

Scalp ringworm can heal in some cases without treatment. However, a doctor should be notified so that the proper treatments can be provided if the ringworm does not heal on its own. Shaving is unnecessary for the application of the topical treatments. A shampoo with selenium sulfide (2.5%) or zinc pyrithione (1 to 2%) used 2 or 3 times a week can decrease the shedding of spores and should be used with certain oral medications. Examples of the drugstore shampoo include Head & Shoulders Intensive Treatment, Selsun Blue, and Selsun Gold for Women. Oral medication such as steroids can be combined with the use of the shampoo for more severe cases of ringworm.

MEDICATION

Scalp treatment for ringworm should be done systemically, or with medication that passes through the whole body, so that it may penetrate the follicle. Griseofulvin, also referred to as Fulvicin or Grisactin, has been the preferred medication since 1958 because of its predictability of rare side effects. The prescribed dose should be taken every day with a meal of fatty foods for 6 to 8 weeks to augment the absorption of the drug and should not be stopped until a culture of the scalp shows no fungi. The side effects include headaches. Healthy children with ringworm are not required to complete liver and blood monitoring. For people allergic or unresponsive to Griseofulvin, other options are available, such as Itraconazole or Sporanox, Fluconazle or Diflucan, Terbinafine or Lamisil, or Prednisone for the first 10 or 15 days of inflammatory ringworm.

SCALP PSORIASIS

Scalp psoriasis is the development of large amounts of skin flakes that have the same consistency of dandruff and occur in red and raised patches on the head underneath the hair. Psoriasis can sometimes clear up on its own but often returns in the future. Psoriasis can occur on the entire body as well as on the scalp, and any outbreak or condition noted should be reported to a doctor.

SEBORRHEIC DERMATITIS

Seborrheic dermatitis also shows excessive amounts of flaking skin cells that appear to be dandruff but usually occurs with less redness and no raised portions of skin. Itching is common and usually occurs on the scalp, forehead, and ears in the area of the most seborrheic oil glands. Fair-skinned people suffer the most with seborrheic dermatitis. Both conditions are treated in the same way, though scalp psoriasis often takes longer to clear.

SCALP TREATMENT

Lotions or shampoos such as David's Scalp Psoriasis Lotion should be applied to the affected areas each night and then shampooed out in the morning. Different products require different application and washing methods, so special care should be given to the directions. The use of the shampoo or lotion should be continued until the condition has cleared, which is usually within 2 weeks, and the patient should sleep on an old pillowcase during that time. There should be a steady improvement of the scalp with no irritation, but less frequent applications of the lotion or shampoo will often slow the results. Since the lotion or shampoo should only be applied to the affected areas, the use of the substance is economical.

TINEA

A fungal disease of the skin, tinea is caused by many different organisms, or individual life-forms, and can occur all over the body but are usually the result of athletic or poolside activities. Ongoing friction from clothes near the wet areas of skin and even remaining in wet swim wear for long periods of time allow tinea to form. Tinea of the feet, or Athlete's Foot, results in itchy rashes between the toes. Tinea and other fungi grow well in moist environments such as shoes and can stay in the footware to cause reinfection. Tinea Cruris, or Jock Itch, and Tinea Corporis, or ringworm, are infections of the skin and result in groin or armpit rashes with dark red borders marking the infected skin.

ATHLETE'S FOOT

Three steps must be taken to treat tinea on the foot. Each foot must be treated with a medical cream before sleeping at night and before putting on socks and shoes in the morning. Within 24 hours, the itching and discomfort should be stopped. The shoes should be sprayed nightly for at least 1 week with a disinfectant spray containing alcohol, any organic group containing OH-, and formalin, a solution of formaldehyde and water, to prevent the development of fungal growth. This spray can also assist in the treatment of foot odor. A splash of chlorine bleach in the shower or bathtub will destroy any fungi or bacteria if allowed to sit overnight. This process should be done periodically to prevent future infection.

TREATING TINEA

Creams or lotions with a high concentration of 1 or more anti-fungals such as Mconazole, Clotrimazole, Econazole, or Nystatin should be applied twice a day to the affected areas on the groin or other parts of the skin. The cream should reduce the itchiness and the red appearance within days. The fungus may develop a resistance to the anti-fungal cream, so some variation in treatment should be considered. The conditions of either form of tinea can be prevented by keeping the groin and other areas that come in contact with sports or athletic gear dry and clean. The underwear and other athletic sports clothing should be washed regularly with a mild or anti-fungal soap. Any rough textured or tight fitting clothes should not be worn underneath the uniform or sports attire.

PROPER DRAPING

Whenever a person is receiving any kind of treatment to the face or hair regardless of the type of service or procedure, that person must be draped with a clean cloth that protects the outer clothing of the client as well as the hair care provider. Each cloth should be kept in a clean, dry area and either washed after each use or thrown away for sanitary reasons. The top of the hair salon chair should be recovered between clients, especially where the nape of the client's neck comes into contact with the chair. During massage therapy, the client should be appropriately draped or covered to ensure the client's privacy and to maintain the integrity of the massage therapist. Most establishments post guidelines about the types of services provided and insist that modest draping be used at all times.

MAKE-UP

The use of make-up in today's society involves presenting an image of trustworthiness based on minimizing any discolorations, correcting any irregular contours, and emphasizing the areas of the face deemed most attractive or compelling. The proper application of make-up allows a person to feel more in control and more beautiful than he or she would otherwise. Different fashions of style demand different looks, and each person should decide which look is the most appropriate for the face shape, color preference, and style. There is a great deal of room for experimentation in the area of make-up since there are so many options available. Repeating the same style or look is permissible, as long as the style or look is what the person wants to show.

MAKE-UP AND AGE

Fashions change regularly and are usually mostly age-driven. As a person ages, the style of make-up or look achieved may change but should be garnered to the comfort of the person and should enhance that person's confidence in the presentation. Being faithful to a simple but timeless look crosses generational gaps, and this style may be the most appropriate for a person as it eliminates wrinkles, enhances cheek bones, or emphasizes eyes. Since most "in" looks go out of style almost as soon as they became in style, any sort of trendy fashion look should be analyzed. The same look at 20 with bright colors and bold strokes may not be appropriate at 40 in a business meeting or out with family. As a person ages, the easiest way to go for make-up styles is usually to the more conservative and classic look.

CLASSIC LOOK

Traditional make-up consists of concealer, foundation, powder, contour if needed, blush, eyeshadow, eyeliner, eyebrow color if needed, lip liner if chosen, and lipstick. Each item can usually be matched to the kind of skin type, such as oily, dry, normal, combination, or sensitive, and to the kind of look desired. Not all people use all of these items every day or even on special days. The traditional make-up item group may only consist of one or two items listed as not all women want or need all of these items to complete the look they have deemed most appropriate for their face or the event. These different elements allow each woman to personalize a look and make some modifications as deemed necessary.

CONCEALER

The concealer covers blemishes and other markings or imperfections on the face, such as the dark circles under the eyes, while offsetting the natural facial shadows. If a lighter texture or color is used, a concealer may also highlight certain areas of the face. The heavier or thicker concealer is used to tone down the natural colors of the skin, such as red spots or freckles. No concealer is needed if the foundation is light enough to even out the colors of the skin under the eyes or across the cheekbones. The concealer should be the same basic color as the foundation but 1 or 2 shades lighter so that the two will blend together. Blend the concealer out on the appropriate area evenly with fingertips or sponge as preferred.

FOUNDATION

Once the color has been selected that will either match the skin or be 1 to 2 shades lighter, the foundation for the appearance of the face should be chosen based on the best option for the skin type. The types available include oil-free, water-based, pressed powder-based, cream-to-powder, liquid-to-powder, stick, shine foundations, and others. Many foundations include some SPF 15 or greater sunscreen and UVA-protecting ingredients of zinc oxide, avobenzone, or titanium dioxide, which is an oxide with two oxygen atoms to one metal or other element. Liberal applications of these foundations can provide some sun protection when used with a moisturizer with sunscreen under the foundation and maintained with a pressed powder that contains sunscreen.

POWDER

Powder should be lightly applied after the foundation to create a soft look. However, not all foundations require powder, such as oil-free or matte foundations or any to-powder foundations. Foundations that remain creamy require powder to absorb any excess foundation or moisturizer that would make the face look too wet. Overpowering can make the face look dry or dull, especially for dry skin types or darker skin tones. Powder should accent the healthy shine of the foundation and give the face a radiant glow. Powder can be touched up during the day to prevent any unnecessary shine. Types of powder include loose, pressed, pressed with sunscreen, and powder that shines.

MAKE-UP BRUSHES

The most important blending tool is the make-up brush available in all types, shapes, and materials. A person may need more specific brushes for a more specialized make-up palette, such as multiple eye shadow colors or eyeliner shades. The size of the brush should match the size of the area being dressed. The standard brush collection includes brushes for three shades of eye shadow, eyeliner, blush, contour, powder, mascara, brow liner, and lipstick. The small wedge brush is best for eye shadow while the large wedge works well for brow liner and a thin brush for eyeliner. The blush and powder brushes should be soft but have a firm texture that holds its shape. The contour brush can be a smaller blush brush, and the lipstick brush should be long and slightly stiff though it may not be necessary to use one. Foundation is best applied with fingertips or sponge.

EYE SHADOW

Coloring the eyelids is usually done to accent the eyes and make them look intriguing or provocative. The look is usually accomplished through layering different colors across the lids in a particular flow from lighter to darker or some other arrangement for a desired effect. The lightest shade is usually applied to just the eyelid or over the entire area between lash and brow. The other colors can be placed in different areas or sections of the eye, such as the crease, the back corner, or just under the brow ridge. The types of eye shadow include powder, liquid, pencils, cream-to-powder, and cream and can be applied with the fingertips, application wand, or brush.

EYELINER

The use of eyeliner to outline the eyes is done to enhance the eyes and create a certain look. Eyeliner is optional and usually accompanies the use of eye shadow and eyebrow pencils. If the eyelashes or eyelids are covered by the eyebrow area, then the use of eyeliners may be superfluous. Eyeliners shape the eye and define it while making eyelashes look fuller. Soft looks do not normally work well with eyeliners, but bolder looks are enhanced and defined by using an eyeliner with the other make-up items. Eye shadow color can be used to line the eye, but other options include pencils, liquid liners, gel liners, cake liners, and powder liners. The colors available span the rainbow but usually fall between brown, black, and gray for classic or simpler looks.

MASCARA

Considered a basic part of any make-up repertoire, mascara enhances the length and texture of eyelashes, and it feeds into the societal appreciation of fuller and longer eyelashes. Mascara can be easily overused, causing the eyelashes to look caked and flaky or hard and spiked. Too much mascara or too heavy a concentration of mascara can weigh down eyelashes and cause them to break. While eyelash curlers are not recommended, their use should be done before the mascara is applied to prevent the lashes from breaking from the strain or being pulled out painfully. Mascara is available in waterproof and water-soluble types with different sizes of wand brushes for application.

CONTOUR

Using contours allows a person to increase or decrease natural facial shadows to give the appearance of more structure or definition. Brown blush tones or pressed powder at the sides of the nose, forehead, cheekbones, and chin can add color, shape, and definition to the face.

Contouring is optional for the classic look, but it is worthwhile for some women and allows a certain kind of intrigue. The use of contouring has fallen out of everyday fashion since it takes skill and patience to obtain the look believably. Often the look will appear wrong from the sides even though it appears fine from the front. Done as a separate step, contouring involves a different shade of powder than that used for blush and is most often the color of natural skin when it has been tanned.

BLUSH

Blush gives the skin a hint of color and health. As a prominent part of the make-up process, blush may be one of the most important considerations in make-up choices and can easily be applied poorly or incorrectly. Most authorities agree that blush should be kept along the cheekbone and away from the eye with the blending beginning just off from the laugh lines and extending to the apple or full part of the cheek. The color selection should correspond to the look desired: darker colors for bolder looks and softer colors for simpler looks. Most faces look best in a more neutral tone that is tan or golden brown. The color of blush should correspond to the color of lipstick. Blushes are available in powder, liquid, gel, cream-to-powder, and stick varieties.

LIP PENCIL AND LIPSTICK

Lipstick balances out the look created by make-up. Classic looks require lipstick and not lip gloss since lipstick stays on longer and provides a more discernible shade. Lipstick colors and textures vary between shades and between manufacturers. The preferred choice of lipstick is one that goes on creamy in an even layer and will not smear or look greasy. Lipsticks are available in creamy, greasy, shiny, or flat colors and have sticky, thick, and thin textures once applied. Different qualities of lipstick such as flashy or iridescent are more appropriate for special occasions, while everyday lip wear should be more conservative. The lip pencil outlines the lips and can make them stand out when the lipstick is applied. Softer lines as opposed to hard points are recommended. The lipstick and lip pencil should be blended together to appear seamless.

FACIAL BEAUTY

Beauty changes year to year, but there are some characteristics that stand out for most people in regards to beautiful female and attractive male faces that can be emphasized or de-emphasized by the hairstyle and make-up chosen. Beautiful female faces are believed to be healthy-colored or tan with a narrower face shape. The presence of fat is to be avoided or de-emphasized, while fuller lips are prized. The distance between the eyes should be enhanced with darker but narrower eyebrows. Higher cheekbones and longer, darker lashes complement a narrower nose and thinner eyelids. Attractive male faces should have healthy or tan-looking skin with a narrower face shape. The lips should be full and symmetrical, and the upper portion of the face should be broader than the lower but with a prominent lower jaw and chin. Eyebrows should be dark, and the lashes should be full and dark.

PERFECT MANICURE OR PEDICURE

All polish should be removed from the nails prior to any manicure or pedicure. Filing should be done with the least-abrasive emery board available and only on dry nails. The nails can be soaked in regular warm water, since soapy water can dry the nails, for any excess cuticle removal though it is strongly recommended that the cuticle not be removed regularly or at all. The nails should be trimmed carefully with sharp manicure scissors or nail clippers with the fingernails being rounded and the toenails cut straight across. The cuticle should be moisturized with an emollient moisturizer, and the moisturizer should be removed before polishing. Polish should be completed in coats while each coat is allowed to dry. Painted nails should not be placed beneath a heat source since heat causes the polish to expand and lift away from the nail.

ARTIFICIAL NAILS

The application of artificial nails is the biggest concern with the procedure. Improperly applied artificial nails can result in nail-related disorders that require medical attention, such as horizontal nail grooves developing close to the cuticle. The damage is related to the drill used by the manicurist to buff out the acrylic nail or create roughness on the original nail for better adhesion since the drill is a time-saver over the emery board. The nail plate can be thinned, and the nail area can become infected due to the chemicals used. A topical disinfectant like Bacitracin can counteract the infection. Onycholysis, the loosening or separation of the nail from the nail bed, is a major concern with artificial nails. Special care should be used when working with artificial nails so as not to damage the original nail.

MANICURED NAIL PROTECTION

Once nails have been treated, they should also be protected so that the manicure lasts longer. The cuticle areas should be moisturized and a hand cream used frequently. Gloves should be worn during chores, and special care should be taken at work. All nail implements should be thoroughly cleaned, and any damage to the cuticle should be treated with disinfectants as soon as possible. Nail products that include formaldehyde or toluene should be avoided, and nails should not be soaked in detergents. Fingernails are not tools or letter openers, and hangnails should not be tugged or pulled. Sunscreen should be worn on the hands and nails and reapplied after hand washing. Nail-polish removers should not be overused, and the cuticle should not be pushed back too far. Proper sterilization is imperative for any manicure utensils.

PEDICURE

After removing nail polish and shaping the nails, the feet are soaked in warm water for a few minutes. Each foot is removed so that the cuticles can be treated with moisturizing lotion and the extra skin trimmed if necessary. Each toe is dotted with oil and returned to the water. A pumice stone is rubbed along each foot to remove calluses and dead skin, and the foot is returned to the water. Both feet are removed and patted dry with a clean towel. The nails are buffed with a nail buffer, and lotion is massaged on to each leg and foot. The nails are cleaned with acetone or nail polish remover to remove any remaining oil or lotion. The feet are patted dry, and cotton foam forms are inserted between the toes while each nail is polished. The polish is allowed to dry, and the foam forms are removed before the shoes are placed back on.

INGROWN TOENAILS

Ingrown toenails usually result from cutting the nail too deeply or filing it too much, both actions that allow for abnormal growth of the nail. When the nail grows into the skin, the skin can swell and cause pain, discharge, and infection. Tight-toed shoes contribute to unnatural nail growth in feet as toes are crammed into a restrictive space. Toes need room in shoes so that they can remain dry to prevent fungus and grow and heal properly. The cuticle should not be cut excessively or pushed back as this can affect nail growth. An infected ingrown toenail should be thoroughly cleaned and the nail be trimmed as much as possible. Overcutting should be avoided as this could exacerbate the problem. Ointments like Neosporin or Bacitracin can be used, but any serious condition should receive medical attention.

CORNS

Corns are thickened masses of flesh occurring across bony areas like toe joints. A frequent occurrence, corns have a small raised bump with a hard center that is painful and most uncomfortable under tight shoes.

Calluses

Calluses are larger than corns and form as a thickening of the skin caused by friction or irritation on the bottom of feet. When calluses become dry, they can crack which causes pain. Corns and calluses are a natural way for the body to protect against damage since the body produces more skin cells to protect this part of the body.

Bunion

A bunion, or hallux valgus, occurs as the result of wearing tight shoes and shows up on the inside part of the foot around the big toe. While there are temporary treatments for these growths, the best form of prevention is better-fitting shoewear.

Hard Water

Hard water refers to water that has a high concentration of calcium or magnesium ions and requires twice as much cleanser, either shampoo or detergent, to reach the same level of cleanliness as would be reached with soft water. The ingredients in the shampoo or detergent can also bind with the minerals in hard water to create a kind of film over the items being cleaned that is not easy to remove. The squeaky sound made when touching freshly scrubbed skin or hair is the sound of friction against the calcium left on the surface. These minerals are also damaging to the moisture in the hair or skin. The most effective way of softening up hard water is installing an ion-exchange water softener at the home. These units exchange the calcium and magnesium for sodium, a mineral that softens the skin and hair.

Saline

Saline is a mixture or solution of one or more salts that is basically isotonic or compatible and comparable with blood or other fluids of the body. Saline is easy for the body to respond to and process, so it is used in many formulas that relate to health or the maintenance of the body.

Cresol

Cresol is any one of the three poisonous liquid or crystal isomeric phenols. Phenols are corrosive, acidic compounds that occur in tar and coal and can be used as disinfectants when diluted. Isomeric phenols have nuclides with the same mass and atomic numbers but at different energy levels, and these combinations are highly active.

Bleach

Bleach is a powder or solution composed of calcium hydroxide, calcium chloride, and calcium hypochlorite that removes or lightens color, kills odors, and sanitizes equipment or surfaces.

Quinine

Quinine is a bitter alkaloid from cinchona bark. Quinine salt is used in medicine and as a bitter tonic.

Formaldehyde

Formaldehyde is a smelly colorless gas that irritates the senses but is used mostly in aqueous or water-based solutions. Formaldehyde is used as a preservative and a disinfectant in many types of chemical synthesis or combinations resulting from elements, groups, or smaller compounds or the decay of an existing compound.

UREA

Urea is a weak base compound with qualities of nitrogen that comprises most of mammalian urine. Urea is one end product of the decomposing of protein and is synthesized from carbon dioxide and ammonia.

HYDROGEN PEROXIDE

Hydrogen peroxide is an unstable compound similar in texture to water. Hydrogen peroxide can be used as antiseptic or bleach. Peroxide can be combined with other chemicals such as benzoyl and used for acne treatment as the chemical kills the infections and dries out the oil.

BORIC ACID

Boric acid is a white, crystal-like acid obtained from boron salts. Boric acid can be utilized as a weak antiseptic but is especially useful as a fire retardant. Boron is only found in nature in combination with other elements.

ALKALINE

Alkaline is a base substance or soluble salt formed by the ashes of plants. Alkalines are made mostly of potassium or sodium carbonate and appear in great quantities in desert or dry regions.

DISULFIDE

Disulfide is an organic compound containing sulphur atoms with carbon atoms. Sulfide binds well with elements that are more electropositive, such as hydrogen, cadmium, iron, lead, and zinc.

GLYCERIN

Glycerin is a thick alcohol-type substance obtained by the conversion of fat to soap. Glycerin or glycerol is combined with an alkaline to form soap and other detergents.

TEPID

Tepid is just above room temperature to fairly warm. Tepid liquids are the easiest to handle, and tepid or lukewarm water is the optimum temperature for healthy hair care cleaning and maintenance.

THERMAL

Thermal is warm to hot. Thermal can refer to the kind of response from processes that require some specific degree of temperature, the rise of warm air, or the material used that will prevent the release of body heat.

PRICKLY HEAT

Prickly heat is a condition of the skin where the area around the sweat ducts becomes inflamed and produces many red pimples. While the temperature of the condition may increase due to the infection, the pimples create an intense itching and tingling sensation which gives this condition its name.

SODIUM

Sodium is a chemically active element. Sodium is naturally occurring and appears as a silver-white element that is waxy and very pliable.

SODIUM HYDROXIDE

Sodium hydroxide is a strong base element. Sodium hydroxide is used in the making of soap, paper, and rayon and appears as a white brittle solid.

SODIUM HYPOCHLORITE

Sodium hypochlorite is an unstable salt. Sodium hypochlorite is usually produced as a water-based solution and used for bleaching and disinfecting.

SODIUM SULFITE

Sodium sulfite is an unstable salt. Sodium sulfite is a weak combination of the salt of sulphurous acid and sodium that can be used for bleaching and shrinking.

ZINC SULPHATE

Zinc sulphate is an unstable salt. Zinc sulphate can be used for bleaching and disinfecting as well as protecting against deterioration and corrosion of metal.

Hair Styling and Coloring

HAIR COLOR

Light reflects off the colored pigments in the hair shaft and present a tone that is seen as color. The shade itself is composed of many different reflections of light bouncing off those colored pigments. For this reason, hair may appear different under natural and inside lights regardless of how natural the color is. The level of color refers to how light or dark the color is as it is reflected back to the eye. For this reason, hair color is assigned a numeric level from darkest black at 1 all the way to white blond at 10. Black or darker shades reflect little light while blond reflects the most light. The levels within the shades also indicate how many steps lighter one color is to another, and this number scale is used in almost every hair color brand.

COLOR TYPES

There are several different types of color. Permanent color changes the pigment in the shaft and cannot be washed out. All colored hair has had the natural color pigments chemically changed, so the permanent color cannot fade out back to the original shade. Any bad color choice can be correctively colored, but this process takes time and money and should only be done by professionals. Single process color can be done in one step where the color is lifted and deposited. Semi-permanent color can color over gray hair but cannot lighten hair, and this type only lasts for a certain amount of time based on the manufacturer of the color. Deposit only color is used as an enhancement and can usually lighten color by one level.

COLOR CHANGE REASONS

Each person should consider what color is possible based on the natural color of hair and what color would be the best for the particular face shape and pigmentation. Experimentation with pigments and lightening kits can result in some embarrassing hair colors, so special care should be taken in selecting a color. Beauty salons receive a good portion of business from people who have tried home hair coloring and discovered that the shade chosen was too dark or too light or in some other way did not compliment the face or skin tone. Changing the color of hair should be a boost to the self-esteem and confidence levels. While the market allows many people to feel they can complete this task at home, more consistent results follow when professionals are utilized for any drastic change to hair color, style, or shape.

CHOOSING A HAIR COLOR

First, the client should choose a favorite hair color, such as medium brown, warm red, or ash blond. Once the color is selected, the current color should be determined by holding up a swatch of the colors available from the particular manufacturer to the hair to see which one most closely matches. A comparison of the two shades, the original color and the desired color, allows the hairdresser to note how many levels of color to go up or down, such as 2 or 6, and the level of color to use, such as a change from blond to red. If the shift is dramatic or above a level of 11, then prelightening will need to be done and should definitely be handled by the hairdresser.

LIGHTENING HAIR

The final color of hair is just the combination of the old color level or base color and the new color level that is added to the hair. Any lightening of the base color will deposit new pigments into the hair shaft and further change the entire color scheme. Lightening of hair involves several stages of coloring, from blue for the natural black look to yellow for the pale blond, that keep the pigment from combining to form undertones of color that are unwanted. The opposite color is added to stamp out the unwanted color pigments, or additional colors can be added to the formula to customize the color tone. The opposing colors allow the hairdresser to shade the hair color the way it should be per the client's request.

PREVENTING ORANGE HAIR

Lightening the hair color results in warm or yellow and red undertones. This mixture, when left on its own and unchecked, produces orange hair. The red and yellow undertones have to be canceled out to prevent this particular shade result. Warm color lightener should not be added to warm colored hair because of the predilection toward the orange. Instead, a cool color of the same level should be chosen so that the warm and cool will balance each other out and not turn into something hideous. The cool color of the lightener will add the missing red and yellow tones and warm up to the final color. A strand test is the best way for the correct shade of lightener to be measured.

STRAND TEST

The coloring dyes can be applied to test strands of hair so that a basic idea of what the final color will be is reached before the entire head is affected. By using test strands of hair, any correction in color or level can be done quickly and with less mess. An uncolored or unaffected hair should be used so that the test color does not interact with a modified base color and produce inconclusive results for the test. The chosen dye can be left on the test strands for varied time, and this change will produce different final hair colors. The test strands should always be checked for any breakage or other damage and should not be attempted on hair with henna or metallic dyes.

ANILINE

Aniline is a liquid poisonous amine, or combination of hydrogen and an alkyl. Aniline is produced by reducing nitrobenzene and is used mostly in such organic syntheses as producing dyes.

HENNA

Henna is reddish brown dye. Henna as a dye is produced as an alkaline from the leaves of the henna plant. Popular with hair color, henna is also used in other dye processes as well.

METALLIC DYES

Metallic dyes are shiny soluble or insoluble coloring components. Metallic dyes can brighten up hair and add more shine.

METALLIC SALTS

Metallic salts are bitter colorless or white crystal compound of sodium and chloride with a metal or a group acting as a metal. Metallic salts are similar to Epsom salts, which are hydrated magnesium sulfate compounds that are highly responsive to change.

HAIR COLORING

Each manufacturer has different recommendations for the best results from hair coloring, and these directions should be followed. Hair should be conditioned a few days prior to any coloring, and a clarifying treatment should be applied to remove any buildup. Before any dyes or compounds are applied to the hair, the hair itself should be divided into sections between 1/4 and 1/2 inches wide based on the density of the hair. Dye should be applied about 1 inch from the scalp and then at the ends. The scalp should be saved for last since the head provides a lot of heat which is insulated by the hair. The dye should be worked through the hair in sections and then rinsed, and the uncolored hair should also be allowed to dry before any coloring takes place. Special care should be taken not to recolor strands of hair.

COLORING CURLY HAIR

Curly hair offers the greatest challenge for hair coloring and lightening since clients have complained of difficulty in the colors being dark or drab or the texture of the hair becoming brittle and dry. Curly hair is fine hair shaped like a corkscrew, and the cuticle does not stay closed because of the shape of the hair. If the hair is not treated correctly, then it becomes dry and brittle. On its own, curly hair is more susceptible to damage because the sensitive layers are always exposed. Any chemical treatment has a major impact on the condition of the hair. If the hair initially shows signs of damage, then the chemical process completed will only worsen the condition of the hair. Curly hair requires special attention and the use of products specifically designed to enrich the uniquely shaped hairs.

CURLY HAIR DYES

The sensitive layers of the curly hair are always exposed, and any chemically applied hair color will soon fade because of this. Any coloring of curly hair should be completed by a professional hairdresser who is familiar with the inherent intricacies. Permanent color treatments should be avoided because of the high concentration of chemicals that are potentially damaging to hair. Semi-permanent or vegetable color dyes are recommended. The semi-permanent dyes are less harsh than the permanent dyes and perform better by giving the hair a more beautiful color that will not fade as quickly. Special care can also be taken for pre-color and post-color to keep the color richer and prevent it from fading as quickly. The appearance of color on curly hair may not be as bright since the curly hair offers many reflective surfaces and does not reflect light as easily as straight hair.

SUBTLE HIGHLIGHTS

The inappropriate way to approach the process of creating highlights is to consider make one large mass of similarly lightened or whitened hair. The highlights in dark or medium hair should be warm and subtle and not overtake the whole focus. The original or favored color of natural hair should be the starting palette as this base gives the color more depth. The purpose of highlights is to subtly introduce a new color or texture. Blond highlights can look too heavy or too harsh as a single tone of color. This color severity shows a definite line when the roots start to grow. The perfect highlight will result in the graceful growing out of the roots and original color, giving the hair a glow and a richness.

HAIR COLOR TONES

A well-processed hair lightening session will result in a color or tone that is deep and rich. The dimension and texture of hair should be suitable for all activities, from heading an office meeting to relaxing at the beach. The hair color tones can be intense, subtle, cool, or warm but should always be directed toward enhancing the individual design, style, or preference of the person. Different manufacturers of highlighting substances can offer solutions to poorly completed lightening sessions, and a less than perfect hair style is taxing on the emotions and the pocketbook once it comes time to repair the damage. Any chemicals or processing introduced to the hair is potentially damaging to the integrity of the hair and should be considered prior to any lightening.

HAIR COLOR COMMUNICATION

Each hairdresser should communicate effectively with the client in regards to hair color or a change of look. Simple color styles in softer blond and radiant ash or light honey can be improved with highlights of shimmering gold or champagne. Shorter hair styles can be improved with hair color that adds in flavor to the face with the rounded contours or splintered ends. The elegance of natural beauty can also be enhanced with rich, full-tone shades of deep black or silver blond, bright red or easy platinum. Hair should appear multi-dimensional, and the right color can give a person an entirely different look. For the more daring, there are options of hair color that are intense and bold while still being sexy and easy to maintain. If experimentation is a consideration, then a person may choose bright bold colors or deep dramatic tones to spice up the look.

BALAYAGE

More carefree than traditional highlights, balayage is a method used by the French to garner more lightening at the ends of hair which is how natural hair is lightened by the sun. The base or roots of the hair should always be darker than the ends, though American highlights tend to go the other way. Bleach or another lightener is painted on the length of the hair without the use of foils. This brush and paddle style of applying color gives the hairdresser more leeway in the color application, making the hair look more naturally lightened without streaks or entire blocks of color. Balayage can enhance facial features by bringing out the eyes: with darker hair at the roots, bolder swatches of color exist at eye level. The coloring streak is less defined and looks artsy and edgy. Touch-ups should be done every 3 or 4 months.

HIGHLIGHTS

A blending of two or three shades of color to produce a more improved natural look, highlights use bleach or another lightening solution to add substance to the hair color tone. While highlights should be maintained every 4 to 6 weeks, they can add warmth to the skin and give the person an individual look that incorporates the rich texture and depth of the hair. Beach-goers and surfers sport this look successfully, with hair that appears healthy and alluring and compliments their leisure time. Professional care should be sought for the natural highlight look since drugstore highlighting kits can make the highlights appear unnatural. Natural highlights generally do not require professional maintenance or improvement as often, and these touchups may be done every 3 to 6 months.

SKUNK LOOK

A more mysterious look may not be appropriate for all faces and professions, but the skunk offers much more than a large stripe of color on one section of hair. With the right hair style, make-up, and outfit, the skunk can add a lot to a person's self-image and individuality. The foils have to be stacked very tightly together to create the streak that is at least an inch wide. Some people have preferred having inch-long panels that are close to the scalp, giving another other-worldly composition. The skunk stripe color should either be a strong contrast or a warm compliment, such as a caramel streak on brunettes or a lighter red on redheads. This style only takes about 15 to 20 minutes to complete but should be touched up monthly.

TIPPING

As its name suggests, tipping involves the color at the tips of the hair being lightened with painted color or bleached with foils to produce a more intriguing look. A few shades difference in color should be selected if tipping is completed because of the starkness of the contrast. The hair will appear trendy and chunky and is perfect for the person with straight hair that has only a little bit of body. The advantage to this experimentation is that the colored part of the hair is easy to cut off if the look does not pan out or the hair can be allowed to grow out on its own. Generally speaking, tipping can last for about 3 months before it has naturally worked itself out.

FIXING BAD HAIR COLOR

Hair color mistakes are always reparable, unless the hair has been colored jet black or platinum. With minor level shifts of color, the right color of hair can usually be restored with a toner or a few extra highlight sessions. Many hairdressers may take pity on an at-home botched coloring job and offer the first session for free. If there are several levels of color to be corrected, the payment will be expected for any follow-up sessions. Color-enhancing shampoos may help offset the color. Purple shades can even out brassy tones, and yellow shades can add warmth to either an ashy or green color. Sometimes just a few drops of liquid detergent can ease the sting of bad color. Hot oil treatments with heat can tone down hair color without introducing damaging agents to the hair.

DOUBLE PROCESS

Double processed hair indicates that there are two steps involved in the quest to reach a particular hue. For example, for a brunette that chooses to go blond, the double process session may be easier and look better than covering the whole head with highlights. The base color needs to be bleached, and then the new color can be added. Double processing is not recommended for people with fine hair or long hair, but the results look great on people with medium skin colors. The roots will need to be redone every 2 to 3 weeks for the color to look natural, and each session will take 2 to 3 hours to process.

SINGLE PROCESS

Single processed hair indicates that there is only one step involved where the coloring is completed with one application of lightening and color depositing. This coloring is for the whole head of hair and can save time by lightening the whole head without using the foil highlighting technique that often takes hours and is very expensive. Single process can give fine hair more body and cover over any gray hair. The best results occur when color is shifted one level, such as dark brown tones on black hair going gray. When undecided on the color, the best advice is to choose lighter tones over darker tones as lighter tones can be more easily fixed with additional sessions. Single process can take about 1 hour and should be touched up every 2 to 4 weeks.

CHOOSING THE RIGHT HAIR COLOR

People with natural redness should avoid warm tones and consider cooler colors light champagne or cool browns. Olive-toned skin favors warm gold or red, though red is the hardest color to maintain since it fades after each wash. Coppery-red looks more natural than blue-red, but each person should consider how much time will be spent touching up color and doing conditioning treatments. Strand tests always help with color choices, and photos of favored looks and color help immensely. The right hair color should add brightness to the face, so any increase in make-up application suggests the wrong color has been chosen. The farther the level from the original base color requires more maintenance, and single process highlights should be conditioned weekly. Caution should be used when moving away from the natural color of hair as most people prefer their hair the same color it was when they were younger.

AFRICAN-AMERICAN HAIR

Different ethnicities encounter differing hair care problems. African-American hair is very fragile and thin naturally. If the hair has already been treated with chemicals or other hair care treatments for straightening or perming, it is even more susceptible to breakage or damage. The quality of the hair color products is most important since dyes that are too harsh will fry the hair and damage it even further. Golden highlights are recommended for more caramel or golden skin tones, while a honey color highlight or all-over shade can complement darker hair and skin. The recommended shampoos, conditioners, and other hair care products used should be gentle and mild and tailored toward the individual hair and skin type.

BLEACH ALTERNATIVES

Rinses and glazes do not contain ammonia or bleach. The rinse stains the cuticle but fades in 6 to 8 washings, and it can be used straight from the bottle. The glaze penetrates the cuticle with a very low peroxide that will not damage hair to deposit hair color on the cortex. Glazes tone down bleached, brassy hair to enhance the natural color by sealing the cuticle and making the hair color very shiny. Rinses and glazes require about 10 to 15 minutes and should be used every few months to maintain color. Lowlights are strategically placed hair color deposits added by a hair colorist throughout the hair to add depth and dimension. Lowlights require about 1 hour and can be touched up months at a time.

BANGS

Different facets of hair and face design go in and out of fashion periodically. Bangs or shorter hairs across the forehead and sometimes along the sides of the face are currently in fashion and can arranged short, choppy, shaggy, or long. Practically all hair styles support bangs comfortably except for extremely curly hair. Bangs need individual attention and can be thermal reconditioned for straight, wavy, or curly hair to give the hair a particular gloss. Regular scissors can produce a softer look while a razor can give fringy, textured bangs. Easy to maintain, bangs can be held in check with spray or other hair care products. It is better to cut bangs when they are dry. Wet bangs appear longer, so the tendency is to cut more hair.

BODY WAVES

With the advances in hair care styling and maintenance, any look is possible for just about any head of hair. A body wave perm like the one sported by Cameron Diaz is a good choice for someone with fine, straight hair who wants a shaggier style. The body wave requires about an hour or so with full schedule touchups every 4 months.

JAPANESE STYLING

Japanese straightening does not involve chemicals that are as harsh as a regular relaxer, but it does leave the hair glossy and straight without having to blow dry any waves or curls out. Japanese straightening is not as dangerous to the hair as a flatiron or regular blow drying and will continue the look until the affected area of hair grows out.

SPLIT ENDS

Everyday routine hair care such as drying or curling will damage the hair regardless of the best care taken to prevent damage. The ends of the hair will split as the result of the heat, the forced air being blown against the growth of the shaft, the sun, and manual styling. The only way to get rid of split ends is to cut them off from the healthier, fuller part of the hair. Regular conditioners and leave-in conditioners help in keeping the appearance of split ends to a minimum, and a conditioning shampoo provides even more help in conjunction. For a quick repair, gloss serum can be applied to the ends and then sealed with a hot iron. While this provides instant results, the process is tortuous to the hair and not recommended for any hair care regimen.

BLOW DRYER

The blow dryer can shorten the time it takes to get ready for the day by quickly heating up cold, damp hair and allowing it to be styled in a few minutes. However, the blow dryer contributes more to split ends and dry hair than any other apparatus in hair care. The heat from the dryer can weaken the hair since hotter things are more susceptible to bending than cooler things. These hairs can sometimes break or separate from the head due to the heat and the forced air. The proper hair conditioning treatment should be applied to hair following the shampoo process to bolster the strength of the hair and enable it to withstand the demands made upon it. Each week should have at least one day of no blow drying or other hair color product maintenance so that the hair can relax and recoup.

CONDITIONER OR RESTRUCTURER

Not all hair care products are appropriate for all hair. A moisturizing conditioner should be adequate for hair that has only a few blond or red highlights that are mixed in with other natural and assisted hair colors. There are several conditioners that specify a moisture-enriching formula, and the hairdresser may be a good source for recommendations. For the more thoroughly blond that stays away from the darker natural colors, the restructurer or repair treatment is a good choice for maintaining shine and health of the hair. The natural honey or wheat protein base can strengthen hair and give back some of the needed nutrients. The hairdresser can suggest the better option for a particular person based on the hair type and the activities.

KERATINIZATION

Keratinization is the process where combinations of sulphur-containing fibrous proteins fuse together to create the chemical foundation for tissues that extend beyond the skin. Hair and nails are examples of the keratinization process.

FERMENTATION

Fermentation is the process where enzymes control the breakdown of energy-rich compounds, such as carbohydrates, or sugars or starches, to carbon dioxide or an organic acid.

IONIZATION

Ionization is the process where an atom or atom group loses or gains electrons and thus carries a positive or negative electric charge.

INOCULATION

Inoculation is the process of increasing antibody production by the immune system by introducing a pathogen or antigen to the body.

IRRADIATION

Irradiation is the process where exposure to X rays or alpha particles occurs. The application of the X rays or ultraviolet light can be used in therapeutic treatment.

HISTOLOGY

Histology is an anatomical study of the intricate organization of animal and plant tissues where the analysis is usually completed through scientific tools like the microscope. Histology analyzes the structure of cells and tissue and their interaction with other cells and tissue.

AURICLE

Auricle is the projecting or ear-shaped portion of each atrium of the human heart. An auricle can also describe an ear-shaped appendage, process, or lobe.

WEN

Wen is a growth or cyst that extends from the surface of the skin abnormally. Wens are commonly referred to as skin tags.

WRINKLE

A wrinkle is a small crease or furrow in the skin formed by the contracting or shrinking of the smooth surface. Wrinkles can be the result of fatigue, worry, or age and can appear as lines, marks, or ridges.

TINTS

As a dye for hair or eyebrows and eyelashes, a tint refers to the resulting color change when chemicals are added to affect the hue or tinge of the hair whereby the cuticle of the hair is raised so the tint can penetrate the hair. This process is defined by the low saturation of color with the resulting high lightness of the tone. Compound dyes combine the metallic colors with the vegetable tint. As a recommended option for light- or fair-haired women or men, tints help present a more natural look that does not require daily make-up application or maintenance. A temporary vegetable tint can be used to darken light hair for a more youthful appearance and will last 6 to 8 weeks. Highlights done well will show a metallic tint in the hair, while coating tints layer color on the hair. Semi-permanent tints only last for about 20 washings.

LYE AND NO LYE STRAIGHTENERS

There are two types of hair straightening products: lye and no lye. The no lye relaxers cause less scalp irritation than lye relaxers. Some people feel that no lye relaxers or straighteners remove the worry from the straightening process; however, even no lye straighteners can prove to be caustic, or able to damage by chemical means, since both types contain substances that break down the chemical bonds of the hair. Both types of straighteners can burn the scalp and head if they are not processed correctly. Lye relaxers are mainly made up of sodium hydroxide, while the no lye relaxers are made up of calcium hydroxide and guanidine carbonate, a pairing which forms guanidine hydroxide. The FDA receives calls and complaints of hair and skin damage for both types.

RELAXER USAGE

Whether a person uses lye or no lye relaxers to affect curly or difficult hair, that person will deal with hair damage if the use is continued for long periods of time or at frequent intervals and without following the required procedures. All hair relaxers or straighteners have instructions on the proper application and rinsing and should be followed exactly. The solution should be on the hair for the recommended time only and carefully washed out with neutralizing shampoo. The hair should then be conditioned to renourish the chemically processed hair. While many people may feel they can process this by themselves, a second person is needed to verify the chemicals have been completely rinsed from the hair.

BEFORE THE RELAXER

No processing should be done to the hair if there are abrasions on the scalp or if the hair itself shows signs of damage. Any dry or damaged hair should be moisturized and damaged hair cut off prior to any relaxing or straightening of the hair itself. Once the hair presents a workable condition, a layer of petroleum jelly can be placed on the scalp to create a buffer between the chemicals and the skin. The scalp should not be scratched, brushed, or combed prior to the chemicals as this only makes it more susceptible to chemical damage. Relaxers should be kept out of the reach of children, and parents should be cautious if applying relaxers to children's hair.

APPLYING CHEMICAL RELAXERS

Different people have different rates of hair growth and different reactions to the chemical relaxers, so there is no exact time to wait before having hair straightened again. Some people feel that 6 to 8 weeks is an appropriate period for the hair to be restored to its optimum state for processing. The relaxers can cause irritation to the scalp and head, so doctors and dermatologists advise to wait longer than 8 weeks if possible. Hair can break or fall out in response to the chemicals in the relaxer or to everyday hair care such as blow drying or curling. The frequency of chemical treatments such as coloring or straightening can weaken hair, and the most recommended hair care color for relaxed hair is the semi-permanent color because of the lack of ammonia and smaller amounts of peroxide.

HAIR DYE REACTIONS

Allergic reactions such as itchiness, facial swelling, and difficulty breathing have been reported in response to hair dye as well. Hair dye irritation can also result in hair loss, burning, and redness. FDA has determined that the ingredients in coal tar hair dye cause some of those allergic reactions, so manufacturers tend to use materials made from petroleum. While most companies do not use coal tar ingredients, the terminology is still used since the language of the law and regulations includes the phrase. The FDA does not have to approve any hair dye. As long as any product containing coal tar hair dyes indicates on the bottle that irritation may result, the FDA will not take action for any irritation. These directives on the bottle should also indicate that a patch test for sensitivity should be completed and that the product is not intended for eyebrow or eyelash use.

HAIR CHEMICAL EXPECTATIONS

A person can use a hair dye or relaxer for years before becoming sensitized, or developing an allergy as a result of use. For this reason, a patch or predisposition test should be done every time before use: a dab of the chemicals should be placed behind the ear or inside the elbow and left for two days. If at the end of those two days any itching, burning, or redness appears, then the product is too harsh for the safety of the person and should not be applied to the skin or hair. After use, the color may also be different from the shade on the box. This occurs due to the base color of the hair. When dyes or relaxers are applied to the hair, they interact with the color already there and may result in a shade far different than what was expected.

STRAIGHTENERS

Any change to the hair or facial appearance is the result of a desire for something different in a person's individual look. Normally, people choose to straighten their hair because of it being overly curly. The straightening process can remove the curls from the hair entirely or just relax them enough that the hair can be more manageable. The process of straightening or relaxing hair is a chemical change initiated to restructure the curly or wavy hair into its straight form. Any change to the hair, be it either relaxing or permanent waving, requires the use of strong or harsh chemicals that must be applied to the hair shaft directly and enter the cuticle.

PROFESSIONAL STRAIGHTENING

The hairdresser is better equipped to straighten hair than someone alone at home. The hairdresser can perform a strand test to verify the appropriate concentration of the relaxer for the particular type of hair being straightened, and the hairdresser can determine other factors of the person's hair, such as the texture, porosity or how well the hair will respond to fluids, any hair damage, and the elasticity or ability of the hair to handle stresses. A mild relaxing formula is usually appropriate for fine, chemically lightened, or colored hair. Regular strength relaxers are tolerable for normal, medium-textured virgin or nontreated hair, and super relaxers are required for coarse virgin hair. The hairdresser can select the most appropriate type of relaxer by the strand test and persoally observing the hair. This same hairdresser can maintain records for any work and make recommendations based on past experience with certain products.

STRAIGHTENING REQUIRED CHEMICALS

Any hair straightening requires the chemical hair relaxer formula, neutralizer, petroleum cream, relaxer shampoo, and relaxer conditioner. The hairdresser may apply the petroleum cream to the scalp to protect the head and previously damaged or relaxed hair. The chemical hair relaxing formula is applied so that the hair can be softened and the curls loosened and relaxed. Once the formula has been allowed to sit for the recommended amount of time and no longer, the chemicals are rinsed out of the hair completely with warm water. The neutralizer is applied to the hair so that the chemicals in the neutralizer can oxidize and restore the natural pH level of the hair since a high pH level can cause the hair to swell and break. The hair is conditioned with either a cream conditioner or a protein or liquid conditioner.

SODIUM HYDROXIDE

As a hair relaxer, sodium hydroxide may or may not require shampooing prior to use but is the strongest of the three relaxers, including guanidine hydroxide and ammonium thiglycolate. A caustic chemical that causes hair fibers to soften, sodium hydroxide causes hair to swell as it penetrates into the cortical layer, or middle to inner layer of the hair shaft that gives the strength and shape of the hair, and breaks any cross bonds. The strength of the sodium hydroxide can be between 5 and 10 percent while the pH factor can be between 10 and 14. A higher strength relaxer raises the pH level and speeds up the processing of the straightening itself. However, the stronger solution can potentially damage the hair more. Special care should be used with sodium hydroxide since it has a high alkaline contents.

GUANIDINE HYDROXIDE

Guanidine hydroxide is a hair relaxer that may or may not require shampooing before application and is usually not as strong as the other forms of straightening solutions. Referred to as a no lye relaxer, guanidine hydroxide is usually less damaging than the sodium hydroxide relaxers or the ammonium thioglycolate relaxers. These types of relaxers can still remove the fatty nutrients from the scalp which will need to be replaced for the health of the scalp and hair. Guanidine hydroxide relaxers usually require a pre-session with conditioning treatments and a post-session with conditioning treatments because of the chemical effect on the scalp. Standard procedure still applies to this less offensive relaxing process in regards to chemical removal and maintenance.

AMMONIUM THIOGLYCOLATE

The ammonium thioglycolate relaxer requires shampooing before application and is referred to as the thio relaxer. Less drastic than the sodium hydroxide and the guanidine hydroxide in some cases, the ammonium thioglycolate acts differently by changing the cystine linkage of the hair in the softening and relaxing of the hair's natural curliness. Ammonium thioglycolate follows the same principles of formulation as the thioglycolate permanent waves and has a pH of 9 to 9.5. Preceded by a pre-softener, ammonium thioglycolate is considered less damaging but still requires the neutralization in its processing. These relaxers can be administered in a cream or gel form and are much milder with fewer chances for hair damage than the sodium hydroxide relaxer.

PETROLEUM CREAM

A layer of petroleum cream is frequently included in the process to protect the scalp and other hair areas that have been straightened before so as to keep the hair from being over processed, breaking, or scalp irritation and burning. This cream is applied over the entire scalp and the hairline as it crosses over the nape, forehead, and perimeter of the ears using the fingertips to lay down the petroleum cream base without rubbing it into the scalp or skin. The base cream is lighter than the petroleum cream and is supposed to melt at body temperatures. Once the base cream melts, it creates an oily film as a protective covering over the scalp and head which creates an additional barrier between the skin of the head and the straightening chemicals used.

STRAIGHTENING FORMULAS

The strength of the straightening chemicals does not always require that a petroleum or base cream be used to prevent damage to the head or scalp and potential damage to the hair. Whenever the relaxing solutions are mild enough, they can be applied without this preventive step. The petroleum cream would almost certainly be required for the sodium hydroxide relaxing treatment as it includes the harshest chemicals in the straightening process. The ammonium thioglycolate straightening treatment may or may not require the petroleum cream since it is a softer process altogether. A protective cream should always be applied at the hairline and around the ears during a straightening process to protect these areas from any chemical irritation. The base cream should also be applied for any chemical touchups.

STRAIGHTENER CHEMICALS

Just hands or another hair straightening tool may be used to disperse the specific chemical solution onto hair that is completely dry. Ammonium thioglycolate, however, can only be applied to hair that is wet. Any hair with perspiration or moisture must be fully dried prior to the application of the chemicals, except for ammonium thioglycolate, and should be combed through the length of the hair before the hair is pulled straight. The relaxer is usually very harsh and should only be left on for 5 to 8 minutes depending on the type of straightener used. Solution left too long on the hair may result in serious damage to the scalp. Hair should not be combed through while the straightener is in place as the chemicals can affect the natural elasticity of the hair. If it is combed during this process, the hair may stretch out and break.

NEUTRALIZER

The neutralizer should be applied to hair after the relaxer has been completely shampooed and rinsed out using warm water only. The neutralizer solution can restore the pH balance of the hair and slow down the relaxing process. As a stabilizer or fixative, the neutralizer can gently reinforce the hair since any chemically relaxed hair will be naturally weaker and will demand careful handling. The neutralizer used in conjunction with the ammonium thioglycolate straightener can recreate the cystine cross bonds in the correct position and restrengthen the hair. After some applications of the straightener chemicals, the hair may appear to have a reddish hue. This can be rinsed out with a special color rinse whether or not the color appears after the neutralizer or after the hair has been dried.

CONDITIONER USE

The straightening process can take a lot out of hair, so special treatments are required to maintain the health of the hair and its texture and straightened appearance since straighteners by themselves can make hair thin, brittle, and transparent. Once the neutralizer has been applied to remove any last chemicals from the hair, a good conditioner can be utilized to restore the natural oils of the scalp and hair that have been removed by the relaxer chemicals. The conditioner should only be applied after the neutralizer solution has been rinsed out and the hair towel dried. After the conditioner has been applied to the hair, the hair can either be styled and air dried or set in rollers and gently blow dried.

MAINTAINING RELAXED HAIR

Relaxed or straightened hair is more porous than regular hair and can hold onto the residue from the straightening chemicals and other hair care products used during the process to its detriment. Therefore, it is important that the chemicals, shampoo, and other products be thoroughly rinsed from the hair. Since the hair is more prone to breakage after the relaxing process, it is recommended to use a detangling or leave-in conditioner with a wide-toothed comb or pick to detangle wet hair and comb through the strands. Relaxed hair requires frequent deep conditioning treatment once or twice a week or as needed depending on the individual's hair response to the chemicals and conditioners.

The chemical process involved in relaxing or straightening hair can erode the hair and seriously damage the integrity of the cuticle. The best way to maintain the appearance of the hair as straightened or relaxed is through the use of effective conditioning treatments. Treated hair requires time to recover, so the conditioner is designed to smooth out the damaged outer surface by encompassing the hair and applying back the oils and proteins removed by the chemical processing. As the hair is recovering from the chemical process, it should not be blow dried or set with hot styling tools on a regular basis. Whenever blow drying is necessary, the lowest setting should be used and an effective leave-in conditioner should be applied prior to blow drying.

RECENTLY STRAIGHTENED HAIR CONDITIONERS

The relaxing process leaves the head of hair more prone to dryness or dehydration due to the chemicals and other hair care products used, and recently relaxed hair is the most susceptible to this potential for damage. There are shampoos available for chemically treated hair types and for chemically processed or chemically straightened or relaxed hair types. Certain all natural, chemical free shampoos are designed to gently cleanse chemically treated hair if this type of product is preferred. With the resultant dry hair from the straightening, the conditioner can affect the strength and recovery of the hair since chemically treat hair deserves delicate treatment. If the hair does not respond well to rinse out or leave-in conditioners, there are other moisture restructuring treatments available.

RELAXED HAIR HOT OIL TREATMENT

Beyond regular rinse out or leave-in conditioners, hot oil treatment can be utilized to restore the moisture and effectively treat the condition of the hair while maintaining the chemically induced straightening. The hot oil treatment can be applied by heating the amount of oil to completely saturate the head of hair to very warm but not too hot. The oils used can be sesame, almond, or olive oil. Olive oil should not be used for colored hair since it fades color. Lightly dab the oil to the roots of the hair using a cotton ball. Afterwards, the hair should be wrapped in a plastic shower cap and covered with a hotel towel for 30 minutes. Then the hair should be shampooed and rinsed completely. It is suggested that the hair be toweled dry and then a conditioner be applied for the best results.

TOUCH-UPS AND COLORINGS

The typical relaxing process can last about 6 months with variations based on the hair texture and growth. It is recommended that hair not be straightened more than every 3 months since only one mistake could result in serious hair damage. Frequent use of relaxers can damage hair, but the biggest problem occurs when people do their own personal touch-ups after the hair has been professionally straightened. The combination of the chemicals can wreak havoc on the hair and cause strands to break or fall out. The chemical straightening allows the hair to remain relaxed even after several washings while the temporary solutions require daily maintenance. The sodium hydroxide straightener is the most popular while it is potentially the most damaging to the hair. Hair should not be colored and relaxed at the same time; the hair may first be relaxed and then colored after 2 to 4 weeks.

HAIR STRAIGHTENING PRODUCTS

Each person chooses a look that best pleases a certain set of criteria, which may require that curly or wavy hair be straightened. Chemical processing certainly can accomplish that, but there are other ways to relax seriously curly hair that do not require chemically altering hair that is frequently not strong in the first place. Environment affects hair greatly, so companies have created seasonal and climate-specific products to improve curly, dry, or unruly hair by removing the residue from chemicals or natural elements and protecting the shaft. While healthy hair can be straightened with little to no damage, hair that is already damaged cannot be improved until the integrity of the hair is restored. Companies have created products with protein and vitamin-based solutions to restore and control curly hair. Once the damaged hair is revitalized, then the hair can be processed chemically if needed.

QUATERNARY AMMONIUM COMPOUNDS

Also known as quats, quaternary ammonium compounds are synthesized from a pure fraction of tertiary amines and crystallized under carefully controlled conditions which ensures a higher level of purity. Quats are used as the preservatives in cosmetics and other hair care products since they have a low impurity content and are easily formed into transparent solutions. Biodegradable and with an excellent conditioning effect, quats do not require homogenization prior to use and formulate into steady formulas. The high purity of the quaternary ammonium compounds makes them ideal for the more intimate of products since any skin and eye irritation is minimized due to the low free amine contents of the products themselves. These quats also disperse evenly and so are effective in hair dyes and creams.

VIVID DYEING

Some people will request a look that is far from conventional because it matches their personality or fits the look they have in mind. Vivid dyes usually respond better to hair that has been bleached of color, and the bleaching action continues as long as the hair is moist. Screaming red, scary purple, and electric blue can be the hair colors of choice and can be added to the hair in permanent and semi-permanent dyes. These bright, unnatural hair colors are chosen so that the color itself will be shocking and incredibly noticeable. The British punk look sports many of these color combinations and fade in and out of fashion with great regularity. The same rules apply with the more garish color dyes: hair must be shampooed and conditioned regularly, and any application of color is recommended to be done by a professional. Acid-balanced shampoo is recommended for tinted hair.

CHEMICAL DANGERS

While semi-permanent dyes last between 3 and 4 months, permanent dyes will not fade but will be pushed out by the roots as the hair continues to grow. While a two-tone look may be acceptable for some, others will request that their hair be dyed repeatedly to prevent this change in color. Dyes themselves contain such ingredients as para-phelylene-diamine and para toluene diamine, which are synthetic organic dyes that are both toxic and can cause allergic reactions in some people. Using dyes can damage hair due to the chemicals in the solutions and even leave a person bald. Many hair salons do not perform allergic reaction tests or insist that any perming and dyeing be done within at least a week of each other for the sake of the hair. Besides allergic reactions, hair dye can also cause pathological changes to the scalp which could lead to cancer.

VIVID COLORS

RASPBERRY

Raspberry Kamikaze is a red-toned purple, long lasting semi-permanent dye that can be applied to long hair with solution left over. This color lasts about 4 weeks before fading. It has not stained skin or workspace and makes the hair shiny and smooth.

PINK

Party Time Pink is not a successful choice for hair color. The dye looks pale in the bottle. The dye does not soak into the hair and results in patches of baby-pink and blond-pink on the hair. The color fades quickly.

BLUE

Midnight Blue is a quality blue choice since the color works well on bleached hair and appears as an intense dark shade of blue. This color bleeds with each wash and can stain the neck and face after each shampooing. Only a small amount is needed to dye long hair, and the color starts to fade after about 2 weeks.

TURQUOISE

Turquoise dyes last on bleached hair for 4 weeks before any fading and smells like blueberries after shampooing. The amount of dye is appropriate and results in no staining.

RED

Flame or bright red actually appears more of an orange color on bleached hair. The color fades after about 4 weeks but usually results in highlights of color from the dye placement.

BLUE BLACK

Blue black is a more goth color that appeals to those seeking mystery and intrigue. The color works better on dry hair that has been bleached and last about 3 weeks with no fading. The bottle usually contains enough dye for any additional touch-ups after those 3 weeks. When applied to wet hair, the color appears thin with some green or light strands.

HENNA HAIR DYE

Before dyeing hair with henna, a harvest test should be completed to verify how the hair will respond to the henna and what kind of time is required for coloration. The harvest test involves strands of hair removed by a simple comb or brush that have been "harvested" from the head. The henna paste is applied and allowed to sit for 3 or 4 hours. The results of the test will confirm the hair's ability to respond to henna. Protective gloves should be used to apply henna, as well as appropriate clothing, towels, and any other surfaces prone to staining. The henna paste should be applied to hair with the fingertips and allowed to sit for the time observed in the harvest test. The hair should be rinsed repeatedly until the water runs clear and the hair is shiny.

HAIRDRESSER HAIR COLORING

A hairdresser should be consulted for any hair coloring or styling because of the benefits of experience. Not only is the mess at the salon and not in a person's house, but professional hair coloring also benefits the client with the skills of the experienced hairdresser and the hairdresser's experience with different styles and colors. A professional salon allows the hairdresser to create a color by blending several different shades if requested and in different steps to achieve a truly individualized color scheme. The hairdresser can do things to the coloring process of hair that cannot be done by someone at home, such as dyeing hair and applying corresponding highlights with a foil wrap. The hairdresser can complete the job per the client's preferences while the client sits back and reads a magazine.

HAIRDRESSER MISTAKES

Even a professional hairdresser can make a mistake in regards to time allotted for a particular step or the kind of color used in conjunction with a particular solution. The condition of the hair can be misjudged, believed to be more or less porous than it actually is. The hair could be underprocessed, overprocessed, or colored the wrong shade. The wrong tone or highlight could be used and could result in an orange hue. The best way to prevent this mistake is to be cognizant of the situation: how porous is the hair? What were the results of the strand or harvest test? How did this person's hair respond before? How did someone else's hair respond to this same treatment? The hairdresser should rely on experience with the process and, if necessary, seek out advice from other hairdressers in the salon.

HAIRDRESSERS AND LIGHTENING HAIR

Clients who wish to lighten their hair more than 3 shades should consult a hairdresser instead of trying to do it themselves. All dark hair colors contain some red pigmentation, or coloring matter in cells and tissue, which can appear unexpectedly in the lightening process and could cause the hair to appear to have an orange or peach cast. Most hair color types require the double process to lighten hair, whereby the natural color is removed from the shaft and then the preferred shade is toned or colored in. The hairdresser is able to handle both steps easier with all the required implements there at hand than someone at home and is better able to advise on how far to lighten.

HAIRDRESSERS AND COLORING HAIR RED

Red dye is a difficult choice for hair coloring since many facial skin types do not agree with the shade and the natural coloring of the face becomes blanched of color. A professional colorist should always be consulted before any changes are made since the colorist can make appropriate recommendations. Dark hair is difficult to style any lighter color, and red dye proves to be just as difficult a choice. Since any hair dye responds to the color already in the hair, dark hair provides a deeper mixture for the red dye and could result in a color not expected. All-over red color may not be the way to go for dark hair types, and the hairdresser could suggest alternatives, such as highlights.

POMADE

Pomade is an ointment used in hair styling that is usually perfumed. By providing a pliable consistency to the hair, pomade gives the stylist control over the final outcome for either a smooth finish or spiked ends as well as incredibly shine. Pomades are available in many different types and can provide nourishment and conditioning to the hair.

LANOLIN

Lanolin is made from the waste products of wool grease and can be used in cosmetics and ointments when the grease has been refined. As a mixture of cholesterol and fatty acids, lanolin forms an emulsion or equal dispersion with water and forms the base of creams or ointments.

OINTMENT

Ointment is a salve that can be applied to the skin. Acting as a protective barrier, ointment can also lock in moisture for the skin by combining oil and water while delivering the medication or specific treatment.

ADULTERATE

Adulterate is the process by which the condition of the substance is corrupted or made impure by adding inferior quality elements or foreign substances. Many cosmetics or hair dyes are adulterated when the valuable ingredients are removed and replaced with inert or less valuable ingredients.

STYPTIC

Styptic is contracting of the blood vessels or tissues of the skin or face. A common example is an astringent, usually associated with cosmetics and hair care.

ATROPHY

Atrophy is decreasing or wasting away in size of body parts or tissue. Skin and organs can atrophy or decline in health in response to negative stimuli or infection.

ASTRINGENT

Astringent is a substance that can pull together soft or organic tissues. Astringents can be used to remove hair dye stains from the face and hands and should be followed up with moisturizer since the substance removes moisture from skin.

UNEXPECTED COLOR CHANGES

Dark roots may start to appear since the hair is growing. To keep from rushing back to the hairdresser frequently, a person may elect to have hair colored lighter than the normal shade. If hair starts to turn orange, then not enough blond was used to color the natural red pigment in the hair. A stronger bleach should be used initially or the original blonding emulsion should be reapplied. Many brands of hair colors are permanent, and a hair color removing product may not work on hair that was colored with semi-permanent dye. Bleached hair cannot be unbleached since the solution removes the natural color of the hair, so bleached hair should be allowed to grow out. Blue or green hair results from a hair color remover used on a semi-permanent color. Bleach can help reduce this coloration. Toners contain oxidation tints, which can increase the red pigmentation of hair.

PERMANENT DYE ISSUES
TOO DARK

Permanent hair dye may result in hair being too dark due to the wrong color or shade being used or not enough time lapse between the bleaching, perming, or straightening so the hair was more porous and absorbed more dye. To prevent this from happening, a lighter shade of dye should be used to color hair or a retouch application should be completed prior to the dyeing. A mild shampoo before the application process may keep the dye from becoming too dark. The ends may appear too dark after the application. To prevent this, the dye should only be applied to the roots and verify the

72

dye is left on the hair for the required amount of time. A mild shampoo before color application can also help in preventing darker ends.

TOO ORANGE OR RED

The use of permanent hair dye may also cause the hair to appear orange after shampooing or more red than originally expected. If the hair dye is too light in color or not left on the hair for a long enough time, this change to orange could occur. A darker dye should be used and applied for the time it took to change the hair color to the proper shade in the strand test. The appropriate toner will help keep the correct color in the hair. A permanent hair dye on bleached hair may appear red because the color itself is either too light or has too much red in it. An appropriate toner can be used or an ash variant of the color to soften the bright red look.

ALLERGIES AND STAINING

The use of permanent hair dye may cause an allergic reaction such as a tingly scalp, itching, or burning for some people. It is imperative that a patch test be completed to prevent any processing with the dye that will cause allergic reactions. If a reaction is noted, then that dye is not appropriate for any hair color change on that person. The hair dye should be blocked from facial skin so as to prevent any staining of the skin. A concentrated shampoo or astringent can be utilized to remove the dye from the skin, and a perfume or cologne may also assist in the removal of the dye from the skin. The skin should then be moisturized as these chemicals normally dry out skin and hair.

GREY

The use of permanent hair dye may not cover grey hair completely if the shade of dye is not dark enough. If this occurs, then a darker dye color should be used.

PERMING

Perming colored hair may fade the color of the dye or damage the hair and corresponding texture. There should be at least a week lapse between the perming and coloring of the hair so the natural oils and nutrients within the hair can be restored before additional chemicals are introduced to the scalp.

INEFFECTIVE DYES

If a dye is added to the hair with no visible difference being made, then the dye selected is too light. Once a darker hair dye is utilized, then the hair color will also reflect the correct shade.

SEMI-PERMANENT DYE ISSUES

The use of semi-permanent hair dye may result in hair that is too dark. This could occur if the wrong shade of dye is selected or not enough time has elapsed between the bleaching, perming, or straightening and the dyeing which would result in porous hair that could absorb more dye. A strong shampoo can be used to wash out the darker color, and the color may fade to the appropriate level. If the hair dye selected is not the correct color or if the dye does not cover over the grey hairs effectively, then a different shade should be chosen that is suitable and recommended to cover over grey hair.

DEPILATORIES

Depilatories are chemicals made up of calcium hydroxide and sodium or calcium thioglycolate that are designed to literally melt away or dissolve hair on the legs and arms. The use of depilatories may result in serious skin irritation and possible burns to the eyes. No depilatory should be used without a patch test completed first. While the depilatory would be used on the hair and not the skin, both sections have similar chemical structures and would respond equally to any irritation.

Depilatories only remove hair at the surface of the skin and should only be applied in generous amounts. The area should remain covered between 4 and 15 minutes depending on the thickness or texture of the hair at the site. The cream should be removed with a warm, moist cloth in a back-and-forth motion as the application of pressure can help in the hair removal.

The hair removal qualities of depilatories should only be used for leg or arm hair and never on eyebrows or genitals since the proximity to mucous membranes could result in irritation. Skin that is sunburned, inflamed, or broken should not be covered with depilatories as the introduction of these strong chemicals will only exacerbate the damage of the skin. The Art of Beauty Epil-Stop Hair Removal cream was recalled in September 1997 by the FDA for causing severe allergic reactions in clients who had used the cream. The adulterated chemical balance of the depilatory showed high pH levels that would remove hair as promised in the advertising but would also remove skin.

WAXING

Waxing can be done to the hair on the body or face with great success. Sticky wax strips can be applied to the skin and removed, or the wax can be applied with a spatula and then removed with a swatch of material usually included in the wax kit. Hot waxing requires that the heated wax be applied to the area such as the upper lip or eyebrow and then removed with swatches or strips once it has cooled. The removal often hurts, but the area can remain smooth for weeks. Once the wax is removed from the body, the skin appears paler than normal because the hair has been pulled out of the lower layer of skin. This deep removal of hair causes the area to remain hairless longer because hair requires time to grow back and will often grow back to a thinner consistency.

SUGARING

Similar to the process of waxing, sugaring uses a cleaner substance that does not require heat to remove unwanted hair from the body or face. The sugary substance used has the same consistency of caramel and is completely natural and organic since it is made up of honey, molasses, fructose, vinegar, lemon juice, water, alcohol, and food dye. The area for hair removal is liberally covered in the sugaring substance, and the sugaring is removed by pulling the soaked swatch away from the skin against the direction of hair growth. Sugaring can be easily washed away and requires less clean-up after use. The risk of irritation still exists since the hair is being forcible removed from the skin.

TWEEZING

By pulling the hair out at the root, tweezing has the same long-term effects of smoothness and reduced hair growth as waxing or sugaring. However, tweezing is incredibly time-consuming and frustrating. The hairs have to be long enough to grasp with the tweezers, and any kind of individualized hair removal process will be painful. The forceful removing of hair by tweezers or through waxing can eventually shut down the hair follicles in that area due to the injury and resultant shock, but this may take years of repeated exposure. It is recommended that any tweezing be done to skin that is warm and moist, such as upon the emergence of the shower. Hair will grow back at a different texture and consistency regardless of the hair removal method used.

BLEACHING FACIAL AND BODY HAIR

An option to waxing or tweezing is bleaching of the hair on the face or upper body so that the dark pigments do not show up as prominently. This alternative can be used on the hair of the upper lip or on specific parts of the face, neck, and arms where the hair is fairly dense. Since the hair is not removed but only the coloration of the particular area changed, the hair will grow out of the bleaching and return to its natural color. Similar to head of hair bleaching, the results can last up to 4 weeks before any touch-ups would be required to maintain the color or texture. The area may

become dry or dehydrated immediately following the chemical change but can be treated with moisturizers or creams. The directions should always be followed exactly to prevent any damage, and a patch test should be used.

ELECTROLYSIS

Hair can also be removed permanently with electrolysis, though treatments may require a year before complete hair removal is possible. As the most expensive option for hair removal, electrolysis can be completed with one of two types of electric current: needle epilator and tweezer epilator. Both use electricity or an electric current to destroy hair at the root. Needle epilators place a fine wire under the skin and inside the hair follicle to kill the root. Regular tweezers are then used to remove each loosened hair. If the electricity used to kill the root is insufficient, the hair may grow back. Tweezer epilators use low-voltage electricity to send mild pulses to the root and enable the hair to be removed with tweezers.

RISKS

Use of any kind of electrical equipment with electric pulses can result in electric shock if used incorrectly. If the needle is not properly insulated, not properly sterilized, and not properly handled, then damage could occur to the skin and hair of the client. Electrolysis work does not require uniform licensing and verification of certain standards to be made available for clients, and 31 states require that the electrolysis operator be licensed with between 120 and 1,200 hours of operating experience. The tweezer epilators tend to rely on the tweezing action to remove hair and not the electric pulses to loosen the hair first. Both forms of electrolysis are not guaranteed as different chemical reactions such as hormonal changes or genetics can initiate the hair follicle to restart the hair growing process.

SHAVING

The easiest and most popular way to remove hair is by shaving. Shaving is probably the easiest and cheapest option for hair removal on the legs and face, but the results of shaving are not always pleasant. The hair grows back almost immediately for some people, and the freshly shaved areas could show stubble or redness or become irritated from the shaving lotion or the dull razor. Using a topical lotion such as a hair conditioner or body wash as the shaving cream with a follow-up of a fragrance-free moisturizer can prevent redness. Aspirin that has been dissolved in 1/4 cup of water can be directly applied to the skin to reduce redness since aspirin has potent anti-inflammatory properties. Dry skin should never be shaved, and moisturizers should be applied after shaving to condition the skin.

LASER HAIR REMOVAL

Laser hair removal has become quite popular since its inception in 1995, so many manufacturing companies are clamoring to have their laser hair removal machinery approved by the FDA and on the market. While laser hair removal is painful and not always permanent, it is touted to be a consistent long-term reduction of hair from certain areas, such as face, legs, chest, arm pits, and bikini area. The hair is released from the root through the application of the laser. Skin discoloration may result from this intensive treatment, as well as swelling, inflammation, and infected hair follicles. Tan or darker skin colors do not have the same success with laser hair removal as lighter skin colors. This type of hair removal should only be done by a professional who is familiar with the research and what options are best for the client.

VANIQA

A prescription-only topical cream, vaniqa has only been approved for reducing hair growth occurring on the face. Vaniqa has an active chemical ingredient of eflornithine hydrochloride, which has been used in the treatment of certain cancers. The side effects of using this medication include anemia, diarrhea, vomiting, skin irritation, acne, and hair loss. Pregnant and breast-feeding women should not use vaniqa since the active ingredient could cause problems for the baby. Per its instructions on use, vaniqa should be incorporated into the hair removal regimen for best results and not used by itself. This particular type of hair removal does not work on everyone and should be discontinued if there is no marked reduction in hair loss after 6 months of use.

HAIR REMOVAL WARNINGS

There are many options available for the hair removal process, but not all people are at a position to consider using a more intense program. For example, hair removal should not be performed on skin that is irritated by acne, sunburn, or some other skin condition. Sections of skin that have undergone hair removal treatment such as facial peels or laser hair removal should be allowed to heal for 6 to 8 weeks before any other hair removal process is attempted at the same site. An additional hair removal process or trauma could result in facial discoloration or scarring. Hair removal should not be performed on people who use topical retinoids, azelaic acid, or exfoliants such as alpha hydroxy acids or beta hydroxy acids and who take Accutane as this could result in damage to the skin and discomfort.

CHEMICAL WAVING

The hairdresser can give the hair a permanent wave or curl by chemical waving or perming the hair for the desired look. The hair is treated chemically so that changes can occur in the keratin structure of the hair to modify the straightness or curliness of the hair itself. While these changes in hair texture or structure can occur with cold-waving or heat-waving, the changes will not be removed by shampooing with hot or cool water. Any chemically induced change will remain evident in the hair until the permed part grows out or is cut off. Hair that is not cut off will continue to grow until the end of the growing period whereupon it will be shed.

"PERMED" HAIR

When the chemical change is initiated in hair to affect the curls or waves, the hair is softened by water or another method, formed or shaped around a particular object, and then permitted to harden up or correct back to its original tension. The softening chemicals drench the hair, which is then wrapped around a perm rod or curler, and heated for a certain effect if desired. The size of the curl or consistency of the wave is dependent entirely on the tightness with which the hair is wrapped around the rod. These kinds of decisions should be discussed prior to any chemicals being applied to the scalp since the permanent wave will last for some time. There should be a review of the condition of the scalp and the hair to verify that the hair is in the best shape possible to be permed.

CHEMICAL WAVING PREPARATIONS

Strand tests are important for perming hair as well as adjusting the color or texture. Hair should not be permed until after the strand tests show no damage. One hair cutting of a few strands of hair can be placed in a hydrogen peroxide and household ammonia solution while the second cutting of strands can be placed in the perm chemical mixture for the time required to process the perm as suggested by the manufacturer. If any heating or discoloration occurs in either sample, then the hair should not be chemically altered with the products available. Both hair cuttings should be tested for tension and strength as well as texture. If the tests show no damage, the hair and scalp should be shampooed and readied for the perm.

PREPARING FOR PERMING

When combing the hair free of any tangles, the hairdresser should endeavor not to stretch the hair as this will weaken it. The hair should be divided into sections and then further divided into neat and manageable parts so that the perming process can be completed with a minimum of extra time required and no extra steps or backtracking. These parts can again be divided into subsections so that the curlers or rod can be placed. The width and depth of the curlers or rods should already have been determined by the hairdresser and client and are also dependent on the texture of the hair and the type of curler or rod selected. Once all sections are completed, the hair is wound, and the chemicals are set to process.

WINDING

Wrapping hairs around rods is the most important part of the perming process. The hair is meshed into sections of suitable shape and size on corresponding implements so that the chemical reaction can occur and modify the shape of the hair. Winding can be rolling or turning of the hair onto the rods, but the goal of winding is to smoothly position the hair and lock the main points of the hair against the body of the hair around the curler for a more consistent curl or wave. The direction of winding is important as the curlers or rods should always be kept in as even a line as possible from the direction the hair naturally grows away from the scalp. Kinks may result from poor alignment, and fine hair is the most susceptible. A good hairdresser should be able to wind a full head within 30 to 45 minutes.

WINDING ALIGNMENT ASSISTANCE

Proper alignment can be ensured by the following suggested techniques:

- Comb parts of hair of same depth while holding them parallel with no tension to prevent slipping
- Hold hair firmly without stretching when lining up the ends of the hair to prevent bending
- Place hair centrally on the curler with the end paper positioned property to prevent bunching and loosening
- Hold hair out from the head at a right angle to the spine while keeping the curler level to prevent incorrect placement of the curls and any irritation from developing on the neck
- Secure the ends of the curler without pressing the closure into hair to prevent bends or kinks
- Avoid stretching hair at all times

While spiral-wind techniques include bendable rods starting at the scalp, the same recommendations are applicable.

LOTION AFTER WINDING

Modern perms include a lotion application, applied by water-wind or post-damping action through indirect application, after the hair is wound around the rods or curlers. This is not a required first step for the process and can be determined by the kind of chemical solution and the guidelines of the manufacturer. Some lotions should be applied before the winding, applied by pre-damping action through direct application. The chemicals will begin to process the hair as soon as the lotion connects with the hair as it is wound on the rod. As not all areas will be chemically processed at the same time, some sections of hair may be over-processed or under-processed which could cause an uneven perm. At no point should the wet hair be stretched.

END PAPERS AND CURLERS

Perming cannot be done without the chemicals placed on the hair, but the shape of the hair cannot be determined without the end papers and the curlers. End papers are thin, flimsy sheets that are designed to hold the ends of the hair in place when the hair is wound around the curler or rod. Preventing kinks or fish-hook curls from being permanently set in the hair, end papers can also be substituted with crepe fibers in some establishments. Curlers or rods are the implements used for cold perm systems that are divided into size and given a corresponding color. The size of the curler determines the size of the curl or intensity of the wave, and the tightness with which the hair is wound about the curler also adds to the degree of shape. Softer waves result from larger rods, while tighter curls result from smaller rods.

GLOVES

Completing a cold-waving process requires several steps, such as shampooing, dividing up the hair, winding the hair around the rods, applying and processing the chemicals for change, applying that chemical's neutralizer or normalizer, and then possibly conditioning the air. The chemicals effecting the change in the hair are referred to as lotions and can be selected based on whether the hair is natural and untreated or bleached and perm-waved. The lotions cause the chemical change in the hair and, as a result, can be incredibly strong for contact with unprotected skin. For this reason alone, the hairdresser should wear gloves to apply the lotion directly or with a sponge, brush, or nozzle that will prevent direct contact with the scalp. If lotion comes in contact with any skin, it should be immediately rinsed off with water-saturated thick cloths and carefully watched to prevent such contact from reoccurring.

PROCESSING

During the processing stage, the lotion or chemical used to change the hair causes the hair to expand, which lifts the cuticle and allows the lotion to reach the cortex or lower skin level. The hair will respond to the chemicals immediately upon application. The processing time should be monitored so as not to exceed the minimum time suggested by the manufacturer. The timing will depend upon various factors, such as the particular person's hair, any prior chemical treatments, the style of waving, the products used to create the wave, the temperature of the room, the initial texture of hair, the density of the hair, the size of curlers, and the winding method. A curler at different sections of the head should be checked every 3 to 5 minutes until a curvy block of hair is evident. At that point, the chemicals should be rinsed and the neutralizer applied.

CHECKING THE PROCESSING

While the whole session requires time as set forth by the manufacturer's guidelines, the hairdresser should routinely monitor the condition of the perming or chemical waving and verify that the times allotted and condition of the hair are still within the recommended time and expected condition per the manufacturer. If the curls are not forming as they should, then the process needs to be stopped immediately and the chemicals removed. The hairdresser should question the client regarding any discomfort or irritation that may be a result of the chemicals touching the scalp or even the tightness of the winding. The temperature surrounding the wound hair should be moderate unless otherwise indicated by the manufacturer. If heating is required, the hairdresser should consult the client regarding any discomfort or sensitivity.

HAIR RESPONSE TO CHEMICAL WAVING

Different initial textures of hair will respond differently to the chemicals. Coarse hair usually absorbs the chemicals quickly, responds well to the change, and is processed thoroughly. Fire or greasy hair will resist the chemical change by not penetrating as quickly and requiring more time to

78

process. Colored or bleached hair or hair that has had recent chemical treatments usually absorbs the chemicals quickly. African and Caribbean hair requires specific preparations and products due to the fragility of the strands themselves. The hairdresser should complete the chemical wave with the appropriate product based on the individual head of hair, and special care should be given to follow the guidelines set for the by the manufacturer in all stages of the process.

CHEMICAL WAVING TEMPERATURE REQUIREMENTS

While the most common cause for failure in permanent waving results from insufficient processing time, the temperature in the salon during the processing can also affect the quality of the wave. Cold salons could slow down the chemical processing, and hotter areas may hurry the process. The natural heat of the head usually suffices for most cold-perm chemicals to process on correctly wound hair. Some manufacturers require that additional heat be employed, and the head is placed under a drier and usually covered by a plastic cap to prevent the drying of the chemicals. Cotton pads should not be placed around the hairline since cotton absorbs any run-off chemicals and holds them closer to the scalp. Any chemicals left on the scalp could burn hair at the scalp level where it is most susceptible to damage. Effective sectioning, winding, and applying of chemicals prevent this from occurring.

RINSING OF CHEMICALS

The chemicals effect the change in the hair by softening the shaft of the hair and reconfiguring the hair's response and structure. The chemically altered hair has been treated with ammonium thioglycolate or even glyceryl-monothioglycolate and wound around an implement to modify the shape of the hair. The chemicals used are concentrated enough to penetrate to the center of each hair and initiate change; therefore, these chemicals need to be thoroughly rinsed or washed out so as to prevent any additional change to the scalp or skin. The chemicals must be completely removed from the hair, scalp, forehead, and neck so that the neutralizer or normalizer can be applied to prepare the hair for the rest of the process.

NEUTRALIZER OR NORMALIZER

The neutralizer or normalizer allows the hair to rebond and strengthen in defense against the softening of the lotion. A weak solution of hydrogen peroxide and a foaming agent work well to neutralize the hair. Some processes require a sodium bromate solution to normalize the hair after treatment. Any extra water should be patted away from each curler prior to the application of the neutralizer as water dilutes solutions. The neutralizer is spread among the wound curlers and left on about 5 minutes. If left longer, the neutralizer could over-process the hair. The curlers can be gently released and additional neutralizer applied to the ends of hair. The hairs should not be stretched while wet, and extra neutralizer should be worked through the hair with the fingertips. Once completed, the neutralizer should sit on the combed-through hair for 2 minutes before rinsing or as recommended by the manufacturer.

FINAL WASH

Chemically treated hair that has been neutralized should be rinsed to remove the neutralizer or normalizer, and special attention should be paid to completely remove any residue of chemicals from the scalp, forehead, neck, and surrounding areas of skin. Some manufacturers may recommend an additional step of an anti-oxidant or a conditioner to nourish the scalp and hair as the normal acidity or pH balance of the skin has been compromised and must be corrected for re-establishing good health to the hair and skin. The hair may then be dried and styled as requested by the client. Each hairdresser should remind the client about proper care for the maintenance of the permed hair and address aspects of the daily routine, frequency of washings, cautions about drying, and usage of any hair care product.

GRAY HAIR APPROACHES

Many clients choose to color their hair as a response to the natural change toward gray hairs. The color shift is not always age-related, though older people have a higher percentage of naturally pigment-free hairs than younger people do. Genetics or the chemical make-up of a person may also cause gray hair to be noticeable at a younger age. The gray hair should be located so that the hair coloring process can be tailored to that spot and not the whole head. Treating just the areas can prevent color buildup and subsequent lackluster appearance, and maintaining the area is easier than the whole head. This can also allow more time between salon visits. The use of semi-permanent color without peroxide makes colored hair shiny and gray hairs appear as highlights. Grays should never be pulled out as this could damage hair follicles.

HAIR COLOR DECISIONS

The hairdresser can assist the client in any color change or patterned style possible. The limit is the client's imagination. Different rinses are available that wash out after a few shampoos, so there is room for experimentation. Before any kind of color is selected, the client should consider the grow-out time. If the color chosen is for a total look, then the client should contemplate how the color will appear as it fades or gives way to the natural color. Hair coloring is often done for years because many people are afraid of what the natural hair will look like after so much time. The choices for color styles are vast, and the hairdresser could highlight, brighten warm, or henna the natural color of the hair. Hair colors can be blended for a special look or certain effect. Well-tended, clean, healthy hair is the most noticeable and best appreciated look.

CELLOPHANES

A new color technique, cellophanes or "jazzing" refers to the coating of the hair shaft by outlandish or garish colors or shades and offer a good first-try for clients wishing to do something different with the hair. Cellophanes do not affect the roots and can be placed anywhere on the head. Cellophanes adhere well on natural hair but are not as effective on treated or very light hair, such as blond or gray.

GELS

Gels are temporary colors that fade after one shampoo and work well with light hair. More appropriate for shorter styles, gels can give a layered color look and bring out natural highlights.

HAIR MASCARA

Hair mascara or hair make-up is a safe way to style hair with colors though it works best on hair that has not been dyed or rinsed with peroxide. Hair mascara works with all hair types and can provide hot streaks noticeable in the evening.

COLOR CHOICES

Brunettes may consider lighter hair or brighter streaks but usually prefer warmer highlights in amber, russet, or calicos of light and dark browns. Blonds usually want brighter and lighter. Gray haired people usually want to cover it or enhance the appearance. The placement of the color produces the most outstanding effect and intensity. The current trend may be toward a double tone effect where the scalp and ends compliment or contrast for the particular look. Colored hair has more volume and body but may feel heavy. Permanent coloring swells the hair shaft to allow the color to penetrate and is fuller. While coloring hair may make the hair more manageable, the goal should be to prevent color buildup.

COLOR ENHANCEMENT
LIGHT BLOND HAIR

Light blond hair may become dull or heavy after daily maintenance and care. For a simple way to brighten up the hair, ordinary or 2% hydrogen peroxide, which should be stored in a cool dry place, can be mixed with lemon juice and sprayed onto the hair. After rinsing, this chemical mixture can give body and shine without serious color change. Pale blond hair should be carefully highlighted, and any prelightening done will lift and lighten the natural pigments of the hair. Color for the whole head should be avoided since the hair is usually fine or thin and not able to maintain any kind of tensile strength or natural tension when saturated with the coloring chemicals. Highlighting is the best way to cover gray hair.

BLOND HAIR

Regular blond hair may also be attended to like the pale blond. Blonds can also apply the molasses treatment by combining 2 tablespoons of molasses with 1 tablespoon of conditioner on freshly cleaned hair and apply this mixture to the hair from root to ends. After 20 minutes, the mixture can be rinsed out, and the color is naturally altered and is a warmer tone. Blond hair can be colored any of various blond shades, such as honey or ash, but the easiest way to maintain the blond feel is to highlight the hair either the natural color or a variation that compliments the skin tone. As a person ages, the hair and skin show that age, which causes the quality and texture of the hair change. A warmer honey tone should be applied to cover gray hair since the silvery tones add years to a changing face.

LIGHT BROWN HAIR

Light brown hair can share characteristics with both blond and brown hair and be pushed either way. The molasses mixture can be combined with three tablespoons of stronger chamomile tea and applied to the hair for 1 hour, being covered with a plastic bag to hold in heat and moisture. This gives the hair blond highlights and plenty of body. The choices for color changes are limitless, and the client may decide for warmer tones or ashy highlights for the whole head or just around the face. Sprays of color closer to the ends of hair or even a more calico layered look could be considered. A semi-permanent rinse in a warm tone just a few shades lighter than the original color should be used to blend in gray hairs.

MEDIUM BROWN HAIR

Henna treatments are always available medium for brown hair without the problem of uneven color as could be seen on lighter brown hair. Henna gives the hair nourishment, body, and highlights and lasts about 8 weeks. Medium brown hair is more susceptible to daring colors such as raspberry or sunflower yellow with cellophanes or gels. The colors lay over the natural color and are only visible if the light hits at a certain angle. A non-hydrogen peroxide rinse works to color hair that is only about 20% gray by brightening the brown and camouflaging the gray into highlights. A visit with the hairdresser should be considered for hair that is closer to 50% gray as coloring is the only option. Permanent color and more maintenance are required, and a nonstripping shampoo and conditioner should be used at every shower.

DARK BROWN OR BLACK HAIR

Henna can be used to bring out red shades for auburn highlights or blond shades for more body and shine. While henna may be acceptable for natural blond highlights, the client should avoid chemically highlighting hair blond as the color fades into copper. Highlights offer the dark brown or black hair a softer, fuller look while not stripping the hair down to recolor it. Color for the whole head should be avoided when trying to get rid of gray. Dyed dark hair has a certain look that is most unattractive if not incredibly artificial. The hair can be lightened a few shades above the natural color, making any gray hair look like natural highlights. If the head is more than 50% gray, the client should consult the hairdresser for options. Warmer colors are the safest choice for active people and those going for a certain look.

COLORED HAIR CARE

Any chemically treated hair will have its own idiosyncrasies or individualized responses to stimuli with regular shampooing and maintenance. The chemicals themselves can damage the hair each time the hair is processed, so color treatments for the whole head of hair should not be completed more than twice a year. By spot coloring or only correcting certain sections or areas, the hair can look more natural and be easier to treat. Even permanent color can fade from simple washing, and any time spent in the sun will affect the colored hair as well. Some hair colors actually improve with the sun, though the sun usually lightens the hair 2 whole shades. The appearance of roots growing out works better with highlighted or warmer hair colors as the dual tones can appear intentional and interesting.

LANUGO

Lanugo is the dense covering of hair. Lanugo refers to the downy baby fuzz that appears on the mammalian fetus.

FINE WOOLY HAIR

Fine woolly hair is the dense covering of hair with the appearance of wool. Fine woolly hair acts as an insulator while longer hair grows over it.

ARRECTOR PILI

Arrector pili is the small muscle tissue connecting hair follicles to the dermis. The arrector pili will contract when stimulated, which causes the hair to stand up on the skin.

CILIA

Cilia is the short hair forming part of a fringe. Cilia refer to eyelashes in cosmetology and the skinny projections at the ends of single celled organisms that speed up movement in biology.

SUPERCILIA

Supercilia are the hairs growing at the ridge or elevation at the forehead. Supercilia are more frequently referred to as the eyebrows.

IMPROVING LIMP, STRINGY HAIR

Sometimes hair can lose its volume or be weighed down by natural oils or chemicals from the environment. To provide extra lift for limp or stringy hair, the client should try a volumizing shampoo and make a point to condition the ends only as the conditioner can add to the weight of the hair. A vent brush or just the fingers should be incorporated into the drying process where care is made to lift the roots and keep the airflow aimed at the scalp. Foam rollers can add body to freshly cleaned hair. A 3/4" barrel curling iron can be used to curl sections in different directions from each other. Using a texturized hair spray can help add some bounce to the curls.

COVERING UP BAD COLOR JOBS

Occasionally a client will misdirect the hairdresser with the result being a bad coloring job. Until the hair is able to handle any additional chemicals being introduced, the client should consider using a strong shampoo such as Prell with hot water since Prell strips colors and the hot water fades the color faster than cold. The next wash should be with a color-enhancing shampoo that is the shade the client would like to see in the hair. A good conditioner should be used in conjunction with these shampoo treatments because the hair is in need of nourishment from the coloring and damaged hair that is poorly colored just looks worse. A hot oil treatment should also be considered. Once the hair has begun to heal from the chemical treatment, the client can consider highlights or spray-in tints to even out the color.

COVERING UP GREASY HAIR

Hair can become greasy and heavy by the natural oils in the scalp, erratic personal hygiene, or chemicals in the environment. The shampoo used to cleanse the hair should contain zinc as in Head and Shoulders and should be used daily. Regular shampooing does not damage hair unless the shampoo is too harsh for the skin type of the person and strips hair of natural oils. Any conditioning should be done at the ends of hair since adding this step to the roots and scalp will weight hair down more. Baby powder can be added to the roots of dry hair to soak up the extra oil but should be shaken out to prevent streaks. The scalp can also be blotted with oil-blotting strips designed for facial treatments.

HUMIDITY PROTECTION

Hair will naturally respond to the change in humidity. Straight hair falls flat while curly hair begins to pouf. To prevent this, a humidity-protective gel can be added before any styling is done. The gels resist the change in moisture by sealing the cuticle, which creates a barrier to that moisture. Once styled, the hair can also be spray with non-sticky hairspray or styling spray to act as another barrier against the moisture. An aerosol spray delivers a more even spray than a pump or spritz which could leave whole sections unprotected or flattened further from the amount of coverage. When the weather changes, the natural tendency of the hair should not also be changed: Straight hair should be left straight, and curly should be left curly. Alcohol-based products should be used over moisture-rich products, and handy implements such as scarves or clips should be kept available just in case.

ADDING VOLUME TO HAIR

The different ways to add volume to hair:

- Add highlights or lowlights as the multi-tonal appearance makes hair look fuller
- Use root volumizers such as gel or mouse and apply at roots of towel-dried hair
- Blow dry hair at the roots with a large, round brush
- Apply velcro rollers to freshly washed and blow-dried hair, remove after 5 minutes, and work through with fingertips
- Use a curling iron on one-inch sections at the crown, lifting vertically while wrapping around the iron, and apply hairspray
- Add donut or cylindrical rats of foam or nylon mesh under hair with hairpins
- Layer hair to accentuate natural wave or curl
- Incorporate simple hair combs or extensions
- Conceal pin-curls under the top layers of hair and secure with pins
- Use rubber bands to make small bushels of hair under the top layer

DEFRIZZING HAIR

Concentration on the scalp using a low-detergent shampoo or one that does not lather too much is crucial. Fine hair formulas of shampoo are preferred. Then the hair should be rinsed and the conditioner applied, but the conditioner should be left in for a few minutes and rinsed out with cool water. Afterward, the hair should be pressed dry with a towel before being combed through gently with a wide-tooth comb. While still wet, the hair should be treated to some cream, serum, or silicone gel, which should be applied on the entire length of the hair to seal cuticles shut. Coarser hair requires richer products than finer hair. If necessary, the upper layers can be pinned to better access the lower layers. Curly hair can be dried with a diffuser. Straight hair requires dividing hair into two-inch-wide sections drying from roots to end pointing the nozzle down.

DEFRIZZING HAIR METHODS

There are other methods used to prevent frizzing of hair and are considered to be tricks of the trade. For instance, shampoo should only be applied every other day since the detergent in shampoo puffs up the hair shaft and can damage cuticles. On the alternate days, the hair should be rinsed with water and the conditioner applied only to the ends. Also, shampoo can be applied only at the crown, and this measure should prevent frizzing by not fluffing up the ends of hair. Once hair has been blown-dry straight, the dryer should be switched over to a cool setting for a few seconds and the whole head of hair dried again.

LAYERED HAIRSTYLES

Straight hair allows for layered hair styles better than curly or coarse hair since layers add body and curly or coarse hair often have too much body for the layered look to appear effective. Highlights or lowlights can be added to the layered straight hair to accentuate the shape of the face and neck and hide the double chin. Layered hairstyles can provide people with long hair an alternative to the regular style since long hair does not allow for much variation. The layered ends of hair can become frizzed or split by everyday means, such as towel drying, blow drying, and basic brushing or combing. Moisturizers should be used for dry hair, and a re-constructer should be used for damaged hair.

HEALTHY HAIR

A great looking head of hair requires a person to have good health, the proper hygiene, and a natural caution toward beauty treatments. The diet determines the hair growth as the foods eaten may not contribute enough iron. Iron is found in eggs, meat, cereal, and beans, and fruits and vegetables improve the body's absorption or ability to absorb iron. Clean hair is healthy hair, and shorter hair allows an easier time of keeping the scalp or the skin covering the top and back of the head clean through regular washing and treatment. While the scalp is impervious to many kinds of foul treatment, it can be damaged by inexpertly performed perms, dyes, bleaches, or massages. Each scalp varies in its ability to withstand reactions to certain chemicals, and the chemicals should be applied to the arm first to verify no allergic reaction will occur on the scalp.

HAIR EXTENSIONS

Celebrities frequently change from long hair to short hair with the hair looking natural. This is due to the hair extensions that are carefully blended to match or compliment the natural hair color. Hair extensions can give instant life to limp hair or help even out a bad cut. Traditionally, extensions last 3 months but have different care instructions than natural hair. Hair extensions should be brushed with a soft bristle brush and tied up during sleep. The extensions should not be colored at home and should be untangled with fingertips or a broad-toothed comb. Conditioners and silicone-based products should not be sprayed onto extensions, and the extensions should not be longer than 30" as the addition of the hair adds weight to the scalp and can damage natural hair.

CHOOSING EXTENSIONS

Price is a big factor with choosing extensions as some hairdressers will add them for hundreds or thousands of dollars. Research and word-of-mouth is the best way to locate a good deal on buying and handling extensions. Applied within the hairline and not lower than the base of the scalp, extensions appear as natural hair if the occasion calls for an upswept style. By not showing the bottom of the natural hair, the extensions are hidden from plain view. The tracks for the hair are braided firmly with no one particularly tight spot. As with anything worn on the body or the skin, the pressure for the extensions will be unnoticeable after a day or so of wear.

FACE SHAPE HAIRSTYLES
OVAL-SHAPED

The oval-shaped face is usually the ideal shape for all kinds of styles. Ovals can wear any style with a certain kind of pizzazz, whether that style is layered, close, full, long, or short. The features of the oval-shaped face make the most important contribution to the kind of hairstyle since certain styles will draw attention to particular features. Bangs can accent the eyes and eyebrow shape, but hair that does not touch the forehead can even out the nose from a side view. The hair type such as curly, wavy, or straight also helps in determining the best style as each person should use what is available to bring out the best in appearance.

SQUARE-SHAPED

Square-shaped faces often have definable edges, so those edges should be softened with wavy bangs down the temples. Long hair styles should be long enough to fall past the shoulders, while short hair styles should be rounded with the height at the crown. When the hair is pulled back and up, soft wisps of hair should be allowed to frame the sides of the face. The presence of bangs at the forehead and along the sides can accent the eyes and eyebrow shape. Naturally curly or wavy hair should be considered to enhance the style, and layers should be considered for straight hair so that the hair will fall softly around the edges.

ROUND

Round faces can best be handled as oval-shaped faces that need a little help for that perfect look. The round-treated-as-oval shape lends itself to more variety and will lift the appearance of the face. The sides should be kept close in which will allow the crown to be at the height of the look. A layered shag is the best choice of styles for the modern round face. If the face is short, the sideburn wisps should be kept close to the face to flatter the cheekbones. Bangs can be used to flatter the eye shape and draw attention to the eye and eyebrow area. Natural curls or straight strands can be utilized in softening the classic look for the round face.

DIAMOND-SHAPED

Since diamond-shaped faces have a narrow chin, the best look comes from a rounded shape that fills out at the bottom. Including bangs that are wispy can turn diamond-shaped faces into oval-shaped faces. The graduated bob falling to the chin is the classic diamond-shaped look. A wispy design for the malar or side of the face softens the edges of the style and adds more intrigue. The bangs can be cut to emphasize the eyes and eyebrow area while the sides can be tailored to showcase the zygomatic arch or cheekbone. No hair on the forehead gives a more balanced look to the nose and chin in profile. The natural state of the hair should be incorporated into the look for the diamond-shaped face.

PEAR-SHAPED

The pear-shaped face looks best in layered styles such as the classic shag where the full crown at the top is used to balance out the wide jaw. Shorter hair styles should be kept above the neckline, and the longer styles should be kept close to the nape. Curls or waves are especially flattering, and any wayward strands can be tucked behind the ears as a defense to keep attention from being drawn to the cheeks. The features can be highlighted in various ways, such as using bangs that are wispy to bring out the eyes and eyebrow area and side curls to draw attention to the mouth and chin. The natural state of the hair should play an important part of the individual look for pear-shaped faces.

HEART-SHAPED

The objective with any heart-shaped face is to simulate width around the narrow chin by using a softer, curlier style with lots of layers since layers and curls flatter the heart-shaped face best. The hair should be full with curls or bouncy waves. The hair should not grow past the chin or jaw line and should incorporate slanted bangs so as to draw attention away from the jaw line. The bangs can be layered or cut in such a way as to accent the eyes and eyebrow area while the hair along the side of the face should frame the face with soft tendrils or curls. If the natural style is curly or straight, that style should be used in the look for the heart-shaped face.

RECTANGLE-SHAPED

Rectangle-shaped faces should focus on adding width and volume to the hair to accentuate the face. The wedge design is the best choice for short hair while the long hair can be worn in a full style to fall right at or right above the shoulder. Layered or chunky bangs that just touch the eyebrows are a perfect complement and can be used to draw attention to the eyes and eyebrow area. The hairstyle can be used to bring out a particular feature, such as the eyes with the use of bangs or the cheekbones with the use of side layers and framing. The natural state of the hair should be enhanced to bring out the best look for the rectangle-shaped face.

WIDOW'S PEAK

There ways to enhance or to downplay the particular look with the widow's peak. Hair should be kept one length to emphasize the dramatic look and provide a smooth silhouette for the hair. Hair can be kept at chin length or allowed to grow longer so as to allow some swing in the strands to best highlight the widow's peak. Parts in the hair should be avoided as the widow's peak looks better when the hair is brushed away from the face.

Layers in the hair or chunky sections at different lengths can be used to downplay the appearance of the widow's peak. A deep side part and combing over of the hair can also disguise the widow's peak presence, and pale highlights around the face can also draw attention away from the forehead.

CROWN BRAIDS

One particular style can draw attention to the face by moving the hair back as a frame. By using a large clip, comb, small covered bands, and an Alice band, the crown braid can add a different combination of textures. The top hair should be clipped on one side of the head to leave the back hair free. A small section of hair at the ear level should be combed straight, and tight braiding with a gradual inclusion of outside hairs can start and be continued toward the back of the head and then tied off with a small covered band. Another section can be completed about 1 inch parallel to the previous braid and so on until the whole front hair has been braided. Any remaining hairs can be scrunched into curls for volume, and an Alice band can hold the hair back from the face.

TIGHT CURL

Tight curls refer to the degree of the curl on the wig enhancement or the natural head of air. A tight curl is a closer curving in of the hair that resists relaxing and can be used as long ringlets or added bounce to the hairstyle.

T-Pins

T-pins are long slender fasteners that can be placed inside the rod or curler during the permanent waving of hair. Usually made of metal or plastic, T-pins are essential to effective styling since they hold the hair shaping device in place without any crimping or bending.

Whorls

Whorls refer to the curling or swirling out of an arrangement of hair or even the pattern of leaves in plant growth. A whorl gives a rounded symmetry to a look.

Swirl

A swirl refers to a kind of motion that appears to continue its curving or twisting pattern. Swirls of hair can be called ringlets or sausage curls.

Growing out Bangs

Bangs may go out of fashion and become hard to grow out. The best way to start is to have them trimmed professionally where the hairdresser can slither or slice the ends to add texture while they grow longer. Wax can be used to smooth back growing bangs, or accessories like headbands can hold bangs back or sweep them to the side. Flexible hairspray can be used to keep the longer bangs under control, or the whole head of hair can be cut shorter to allow the hair to grow at the same rate to even out the length. A volumizing spray and a round brush can be used in the blow-drying of longer bangs to give lift and shape. The bangs can be pulled straight back and help in place with a barrette or cut at an angle so the bangs blend in with the rest of the hair.

Initial Hair Consultation

Some people decide a haircut is the most logical choice for changing a look or updating a style but have no idea what they want the new look or style to be. Photos can be brought in or selected from magazines at the front of the salon to give the hairdresser an idea of what particular look or cut is preferred. A discussion can center around what is not liked about the current style but what features are important to the person so the cut can emphasize those features. The face shape will be analyzed since certain looks do not flatter every face. The hairdresser can assess the texture and length of the curly hair and how much work the person is willing to do to maintain a particular look. The hair may be shampooed or spritzed with water before the cutting begins.

Trade Tools

Most hairdressers have a variety of tools to complete any job. The hair can be cut with scissors, shears, electric hair clippers, hand hair clippers, and razors. Scissors are available in different grips and sizes for a comfortable fit for the hairdresser and can range in price from $10 to $600 depending on the quality of the brand. Shears are scissors with teeth-like edges that can give a less severe cut to the ends of hair and may be better suited for layers or fringe bangs. Electric hair clippers can effectively shorten the short hairs for both men and women with little to no damage to the scalp if used correctly. Hand hair clippers are more old-fashioned looking but can be used for closer work. Razors offer a choppy look for hair and are usually incorporated with facial shaving.

Professional Look

Proper styling for any look can make it smooth and neat for any professional. However, the bob can improve almost any look if styled correctly and can mature a youthful style as well as relaxing a formidable style. All hair lengths and types can wear the bob and have it be flattering to the facial shape, and the bob can be easily corrected to sleek, straight, wavy, or textured as needed. The hair should be tapered to a fine edge that blends into the jaw line for the graduated bob. The hairdresser can use either a razor or set of trimming shears to remove some of the bulk of the hair o give thick hair a more airy feeling. This can emphasize eyes and cheeks and is easily pulled back for a more carefree style.

BEST TIPS FOR HAIR TYPES
CURLY HAIR

Curly hair can be maintained and nourished through simple steps. Moisturizing curly hair can improve the look and make it more manageable to style. The curly hair should not be blow-dried until it is about 90% dry since the use of forced heat will make it expand and frizz up. A diffuser can be used on the drier to keep the frizz down, and the fingers can be used to style the dry or almost-dry hair. The dry curls can be set with a blast of cold air from the drier, and the flyaway strands can be smoothed down with serum, oil, or cream that is massaged through the hair.

DAMAGED HAIR

Damaged hair should be allowed to repair in as effective a way as possible. Therefore, freshly shampooed and conditioned damaged hair should be allowed to air dry frequently to give the strands time to restore moisture. Styling products such as flat irons and curling irons should be avoided for regular use, and any blow-drying done should done with a hair-dryer that has a nozzle so that distance can be made between the hair and the heat. It is recommended that cool heat be used when drying damaged hair. Regular use of conditioners should also be incorporated as the conditioners can supply moisture and help build the natural elasticity in the hair. Other products such as hot oil treatments and other protein-rich lotions for damaged hair can aid the restoration of the hair.

THIN HAIR

Thin hair usually needs more lift to improve its look. A volumizing shampoo and conditioner can be used in conjunction with mouse and holding hairspray to maintain shape and texture. Other hair care products such as serums, creams, pomades, and other oils can weigh the hair down and flatten the look. Any drying should be done to hair that has been flipped over with the dryer pointed at the underside of hair. This method can add lift and volume. Rollers, curling irons, and fat round brushes can also be used to add curls or waves to give the hair more movement. Highlights in the correct places or even all-over color can also add body since the reflecting light can create the illusion of more hair.

THICK HAIR

Thicker hair can be hot, heavy, and very uncomfortable for some people. This type of hair needs to be professionally treated frequently to keep the growth from going out of control and becoming difficult to manage. Long layers can be cut in the hair as this will decrease the quantity of hair and minimize the sheer bulk size. Serums, creams, pomades, and other oils can keep the hair more closely contained which will allow the tresses to appear not as full. Utensils such as hair bands or ponytail holders can certainly assist in keeping hair in check. Special care should be given to the ends as they tend to become frizzy which could add bulk.

PHARMACOLOGY

Pharmacology refers to the scientific study of medical drugs, toxicology, and other therapeutic options for repairing and maintaining health of the body and its associated parts, as well as the reactions and properties of the medicines and chemicals with their relationship to the treatments. As medicines and chemicals are created, they are analyzed to determine the kind of care possible based on the use of a particular regimen. The options and choices are always being improved with study. An abstract published every 5 years, the United States Pharmacopoeia allows for the FDA

88

and the US Drug Enforcement Administration to enforce any necessary actions for the medical and physical treatments created and proffered for public and private consumption.

OXYMELANIN

Oxymelanin refers to the conversion of the natural melanin pigment in hair when that hair becomes bleached. Since the bleach breaks down the molecules reflecting brown and black colors, the oxymelanin molecules which are smaller allow the lighter colors of blond or red to show through the hair in the hair-lightening process.

NAPHTHA

Naphtha can refer to several active and often flammable hydrocarbon mixtures in liquid form that are used as solvents and in the dilution of other chemicals. Naphtha can be used in cleaning solvents and fluids.

NITRITE

Nitrite refers to the salt or ester of nitrous acid and can be used in dye manufacturing. As a flammable liquid, nitrite is combined with amyl alcohol and used commercially in dyeing and preserving.

SEASON WEATHER CHANGES

The hairdresser is the best person to suggest a new look for the change in season as well as a healthy start on fixing the winter hair. The damaged ends should be trimmed away while the new hair should be treated for any style considerations. The bangs should be considered, and layers could be suggested. Curls often make this transition easy. The hair should be moisturized and smoothed after the hard winter months with deep conditioning treatments that will smooth the cuticles and add the nourishment back to the scalp and hair. Certain hairstyles are more effective for the weather change, such as ponytails or buns where the hair is held back from the head and off the neck.

HARMFUL SUMMER CHEMICALS

Long exposure to the sun and other summer-related chemicals like chlorine and salt water can really damage hair that is unprotected by removing any moisture, drying out strands, and fading or changing the color. There are hair sunscreens available to aid in the protection of the hair in addition to the skin so that the sun rays will not completely undo or destroy any color change made for the season. Hats including baseball caps or scarf-tied floppy covers can also be worn to protect the hair and the more sensitive skin of the face from harmful rays. Whenever hair is doused in chlorine or salt water, it should be thoroughly rinsed immediately afterward so as to prevent any permanent change in coloration.

FINGER DRYING HAIR

A blow dryer can be used on dry or damaged hair but is only recommended at the lowest setting and with a cold blast. Finger drying hair is the preferred method to dry hair that is damaged or dry or to create a wavier look in short hair that is naturally curly. The hair should be shampooed and conditioned as normal, sprayed with gel, and combed through. The fingertips can be run upwards and forwards through the hair from the root to the end in a rapid motion. The hair should be lifted at the crown to get more height at the roots, and this motion should be continued as the hair dries. The hair at the sides can also be flattened with the fingertips so as to balance out the look.

BLOW DRYING LONG HAIR

After shampooing and conditioning, the hair can be combed with a wide-tooth comb to remove tangles and partially dried to remove any excess moisture. A handful of mousse can be spread through hair and evenly distributed from tip to end. The hair is then divided into 2 sections with the top and sides clipped. The root area should be dried first with hair brushed from roots to ends, curving at the ends for a slight bend, until the hair is dried. Other sections can be released and dried the same way until all hair is dry. Serum can be applied through the hair to flatten any stray ends. The hair may again be dried roots to ends with the drier pointing downwards to prevent any damage to the cuticle and encourage shine.

WIGS

Wigs and hair replacements are available in several styles and colors and by several manufacturers and designers. The standard distinction between wigs includes length, color, cap construction, and cap size. Facial analysis is the best way to start with wig selection as not all wigs and corresponding styles will flatter all face shapes. The same shape descriptions, such as round, oval, square, pear, diamond, heart, and oblong, apply for the hair and style selection. The length can be chin, short, long, or medium, and color can also include gray hairpieces. Cap construction can refer to monofilament wigs or capless wigs, while cape size can refer to petite, average, large, and extra large.

HUMAN HAIR WIGS

Wigs and hair replacements can be necessary for a preferred style or to allow damaged hair to grow back to its original quality. Human hair wigs are often preferred over synthetic hair wigs since the style is more natural and less noticeable as a wig. Human hair wigs made of a soft touch brand of hair can be washable as well as settable. Machine created for comfort and durability, human hair wigs can feature monofilament hand-tied tops that can be parted or brushed in any direction. The lining for the cap can also be in velvet or other soft materials to prevent any friction with the scalp and are sized for the type of head, such as petite or average, per the manufacturer.

CHOOSING A HAIRPIECE

Used as an extension or to add volume to existing hair, the hairpiece should be matched to the shade of the original hair as closely as possible so the hair looks natural and does not appear to be out of place. Lighter colored hair may be selected while any darker shades should be avoided as hair can be lightened by the sun and other kinds of exposures but never darkened naturally. The hair should also match the quality of the hair, as straight locks added to naturally curly hair could undo the effect desired for the look. The hairpiece can be specially dyed if there is no color available that matches. Under those circumstances, a section or sample of the hair will need to be sent in to the specific manufacturer.

MAINTAINING A WIG

Wigs must be stored and cleaned between wearings and if any damage occurs. There are wig stands to hold the wig in its shape when not being worn and are usually wire or plastic frames that can be collapsed for easy storage and travel. Hair cap retainers and wig liners can protect the scalp and the wig from any friction or irritation, and special tapes can be used to hold the wig in place at certain points on the scalp. Mild shampoos can remove any environmental damage as well as any scalp oils, while conditioners can be specifically designed for the type of wig and help maintain the shiny healthy look. Special brushes with anti-static bristles and smaller brushes with silicone tips are available, and other items such as mousse and hairspray can be used for wig styling.

FITTING WIGS

Most people who are looking for wigs or hair replacements are embarrassed and sensitive about being there in the first place. Most hair replacement clients are looking to cover up thinning hair or just maintain a professional image after serious medical procedures such as chemotherapy. Since the client is already hesitant, the hairdresser should be patient while conferring with the client in a private room to discuss options for the kind of wig. Books and pamphlets can be a good discussion piece as the client makes selections. Once a wig is chosen, the client's hair should be secured under a wig cap or liner and made completely flat with either wrapped hair or pin curls so that the wig can fit securely on the head. The wig manufacturer will have directions on adhering the hairpiece to the scalp. The correct wig will make the client feel normal and beautiful.

FRENCH BRAIDS

The French braid is a classic style that can be completed in easy steps:

- Place thumbs above and slightly behind the shell of the ear and draw hair back and up to the crown in a ponytail
- Braid hair left strand over center and then right over center to hold the braid in place
- Hold the braid in one hand while keeping the three sections separated with the fingers and use the other hand to bring in a section of hair half as thick as the original
- Add the extra hair to the braiding with each pass and keep the three sections separated with the fingers
- Continue the same process for both sides, adding the hair to the braid as it progresses down the back of the head
- Braid the remaining loose hairs in a traditional English braid

FISHTAIL BRAIDS

While fishtail braids are basically the same as French braids, the difference is that fishtail braids are composed of two strands and created at the base of the originally formed ponytail. The sections should be formed in equal thickness and pulled tightly during the braiding, and fishtail braids work best on dry, medium to long hair that is not layered. The steps are:

- The ponytail should be divided into 2 equal sections and a small section from underneath the left side should be crossed over the right side and pulled tight
- One hand should hold the braid and keep the sections separated by the fingers
- A small section from the right side should be crossed over the left side and pulled tight
- The crossing over should continue until the end of the hair, and that should be secured with an elastic band

Cosmetology Practice Test

Want to take this practice test in an online interactive format?
Check out the bonus page, which includes interactive practice questions and
much more: **http://www.mometrix.com/bonus948/cosmetology**

1. How might the skin's surface appear following the application of a product with a pH balance of 4?

   a. Red
   b. Smooth
   c. Chafed
   d. Dry

2. Which of the following types of electric therapy aids in the process of desincrustation?

   a. Use of ultraviolet current
   b. Use of an anode
   c. Use of galvanic current
   d. Use of a cathode

3. Why might the use of prednisone be a contraindication for a facial service?

   a. It causes the skin to thin
   b. It removes the top layer of the skin
   c. It causes the skin to be inflamed/irritated
   d. It causes broken capillaries

4. The following condition causes the nail to shrink in size and separate from the nail bed.

   a. Onychatrophia
   b. Paronychia
   c. Onychogryphosis
   d. Leukonychia

5. What scalp disorder is characterized by red, itchy, and watery blisters?

   a. Tinea capitis
   b. Scabies
   c. Pustules
   d. Excoriation

6. Of the following options, nail polish remover has which of the following pH ranges?

   a. 5-6
   b. 6-7
   c. 8-9
   d. 9-10

7. A sloughing lotion is:

   a. The first product that should be applied to the feet during a pedicure.
   b. Used to eliminate toxins from the skin during a pedicure.
   c. Used to remove dead skin cells from the skin's surface during a pedicure.
   d. Used to eliminate callouses during a pedicure.

8. Of the following methods listed, which is the most accurate for determining the pH of a shampoo?

   a. Use of a pH meter
   b. Use of a pH pencil
   c. Use of Nitrazine
   d. Use of a hydrometer

9. What portion of the hair structure supplies nourishment to its surrounding germinal matrix cells?

   a. Cortex
   b. Hair bulb
   c. Papilla
   d. Medulla

10. A cornrow braid is created by which of the following techniques?

   a. Standard braid
   b. Dutch braid
   c. French braid
   d. Fishtail braid

11. Which of the following ingredients might be found in a conditioner to combat static in hair?

   a. Amines/quats
   b. Thioglycolic acid
   c. Fatty acids
   d. Dimethicone

12. What is the technical name for the part of the cutting tool upon which a technician's ring finger or pinky finger rests?

   a. Finger rest
   b. Balancer
   c. Foot
   d. Tang

13. What chemical is responsible for the swelling of the hair during a chemical relaxer?

   a. Sodium perborate
   b. Hydrogen peroxide
   c. Glyceryl monothioglycolate
   d. Ammonium hydroxide

14. What is the main purpose of a Wood's lamp in a facial?
   a. To provide light
   b. To provide magnification
   c. To provide soothing heat
   d. To provide ultraviolet light

15. The technical name for a blackhead is a _____.
   a. Pustule
   b. Milia
   c. Papule
   d. Comedo

16. A wooden nail file has come into contact with a patron's blood. What is the minimal method of infection control that must be taken before it can be reused?
   a. Sterilization via broad spectrum disinfectant
   b. Sterilization via submersion
   c. The nail file cannot be reused.
   d. Disinfection via submersion

17. The _____ is the active tissue of the nail that generates cells.
   a. Perionychium
   b. Nail matrix
   c. Eponychium
   d. Hyponychium

18. How can a scalp massage affect a client's hair growth?
   a. It relaxes the client
   b. It stimulates the scalp
   c. It allows the conditioner to penetrate more thoroughly
   d. It does not affect a client's hair growth

19. Which of the following techniques used in cutting short hair results in hair gradually going from a longer length to a shorter one?
   a. Blunt technique
   b. Uniform layered technique
   c. Graduated technique
   d. Long layered technique

20. Claire is seeking a hair color result that will alter the tone of her hair without causing chemical damage. Which of the following options would be best for her?
   a. Semi-permanent hair color
   b. Henna
   c. Temporary hair color
   d. Demi-permanent hair color

21. How long does it take for skin cells to complete the process of keratinization?

    a. 25-30 days

    b. Two weeks

    c. 60 days

    d. Overnight, or during a resting period

22. When forming acrylic nails, which of the following statements would be correct?

    a. The middle of the nail should contain the thickest layer of acrylic.

    b. The area closest to the cuticle should contain the thickest layer of acrylic.

    c. The free edge should contain the least amount of acrylic.

    d. The acrylic should be evenly distributed from the cuticle area to the free edge.

23. _____ is used to destroy or kill all microbes on a surface.

    a. Bleach

    b. Disinfectant

    c. Germicide/virucide

    d. Sterilant

24. How can "cutting past the second knuckle" affect the outcome of hair design?

    a. It causes the hair to bunch up

    b. It can cause injury

    c. It lessens the tension

    d. It can cause the shears to unevenly wear

25. Intensity of hair color refers to which of the following?

    a. Its ability to lighten

    b. The vibrancy of the pigment

    c. The amount of pigment

    d. The volume of the developer

26. Felicia has her nail technician buff the tops of her toenails to eliminate ridges. What order of operation should her technician use?

    a. Medium-grit nail file, fine-grit nail file, nail buffer

    b. Fine-grit nail file, nail buffer

    c. Foot file, medium-grit nail file, nail buffer

    d. Medium-grit mechanical file, fine-grit mechanical file, nail buffer

27. Why is it recommended that a chelating shampoo be used prior to a permanent waving service?

    a. To remove surface and chemical buildup

    b. To remove oil and debris from the hair

    c. To normalize the pH of the hair

    d. To aid in the wrapping process

28. Michelle arrives for her wedding day hair appointment with clean, dry hair. Which of the following tools would be most appropriate for creating curls?

    a. Velcro rollers
    b. Rollers
    c. A Marcel iron
    d. Double-prong clip

29. Which of the following ingredients might be added to a shampoo used to strengthen hair?

    a. Lipid
    b. An astringent
    c. Keratin
    d. Glycerol

30. What causes the hair to visibly lighten when high-lift hair color or bleach is applied to the hair strand?

    a. Dissolvement of pigment
    b. Diffusion of pigment
    c. Neutralization of pigment
    d. Division of pigment

31. _____ would NOT be considered an acidic substance.

    a. Perm neutralizer
    b. Saliva
    c. Vinegar
    d. Blood

32. When contouring is used in a makeup application, which principle of light is applied?

    a. Drawing attention away from the feature
    b. Drawing attention towards the feature
    c. Making the feature appear larger
    d. Making the feature appear smaller

33. Proper exfoliation can help to minimize which of the following skin conditions?

    a. Eczema
    b. Milia
    c. Psoriasis
    d. Steatoma

34. What is the most effective form of infection control for any lancets/needles involved in a facial process?

    a. Use of an EPA-registered disinfectant
    b. Use of an EPA-registered sterilant
    c. Use of hot soapy water
    d. Use of disposable implements

35. What is one of the benefits of using vibration as part of a facial service?

    a. To increase muscle tone
    b. To increase glandular activity
    c. To decrease sebum production
    d. To reduce a client's stress

36. Which of the following manual tools always has a replaceable blade?

    a. Thinning shears
    b. Razor
    c. Clippers
    d. Neck trimmer

37. A callus-softening product should be used _____.

    a. After soaking the affected area
    b. On dry skin
    c. Prior to using a foot file
    d. In accordance with manufacturer's direction

38. Which of the following is disinfection incapable of doing?

    a. Killing viruses
    b. Killing tuberculosis
    c. Killing bacterial spores
    d. Killing pseudomonas

39. A blending shear has how many teeth?

    a. 5-9
    b. 14-19
    c. 38-50
    d. 26-30

40. What is the purpose of an emulsifier in shampoo?

    a. To create lather
    b. To modify consistency
    c. To create friction, which loosens oil and debris
    d. To bond together otherwise unmixable substances

41. Which of the following hair types would be most suitable for a higher heat setting on a thermal tool?

    a. Permed hair
    b. Brown hair
    c. Coarse/curly hair
    d. Wavy hair

42. Why is it recommended to color hair after a relaxer service and not before it?

    a. To add vibrancy
    b. To minimize the risk of damage
    c. To minimize the risk of fading
    d. To contribute conditioning agents

43. **What is the first step a technician should take if they cut themselves?**

    a. Wash with soap and water
    b. Apply an anticoagulant
    c. Apply firm pressure to stop the bleeding
    d. Apply an antiseptic

44. **What is the technical name used for holding shears in a manner in which they are not open and not facing the client?**

    a. Cupping
    b. Palming
    c. Guarding
    d. Locking

45. **While providing a facial, what is the proper distance a technician should keep the steamer away from a client's face?**

    a. 12-14 inches
    b. 16-18 inches
    c. 8-10 inches
    d. 18-20 inches

46. **Which of the following might be used in a facial to minimize the appearance of larger pores?**

    a. An exfoliant
    b. A clay-based mask
    c. An alginate mask
    d. A moisturizer

47. **What characteristic might hair have which would make it most susceptible to static electricity?**

    a. Coarse
    b. Thin
    c. Wavy
    d. Fine

48. **What type of hair color service would be best for a client wishing to cover grey hair while maintaining the same tone and level of hair?**

    a. Permanent hair color
    b. Semi-permanent hair color
    c. Bleach
    d. Deposit-only hair color

49. **_____ is a condition that causes an increased curvature of the nails.**

    a. Onychogryphosis
    b. Onycholysis
    c. Onychauxis
    d. Onychomycosis

50. Tina's pointer finger is warm to the touch and swollen. Which of the following conditions might cause these symptoms?

a. Paronychia
b. Onycholysis
c. Tinea
d. Onychia

51. Why is bleach NOT the best choice for immersion of shears following exposure to blood?

a. It is ineffective
b. It can cause chemical reactions with other chemicals
c. It must be diluted
d. It can corrode

52. What is the purpose of waving lotion in an exothermic permanent wave?

a. To provide grip on the perm rods
b. To create a medium for heat
c. To create waves
d. To break down the structure of the hair for re-forming

53. Which of the following conditions is characterized by redness of the skin?

a. Rosacea
b. Chloasma
c. Melanoderma
d. Vitiligo

54. When shaping eyebrows, which point of reference of the eye should be used when determining proper positioning of the arch?

a. The pupil
b. The iris
c. The outer corner
d. The inner corner

55. Which of the following is the most productive way of slowing the spread of bacteria in a salon or spa setting?

a. Bleaching towels and capes between each use
b. Washing hands
c. Disinfecting stylist chair between each use
d. Storing disinfected combs and brushes in a closed container

56. Which of the following lengths would best suit a client who desires to minimize attention to her long face?

a. Hair cut at collarbone
b. Chin-length bob
c. Diagonal forward lob
d. Pixie cut

57. Which of the following statements is INCORRECT?

a. Without a guard or comb, a clipper is capable of removing hair to varying lengths
b. The moving blade on a clipper is known as the heel
c. A razor cuts the end of hair to an angle
d. Slithering is done with a razor

58. Which of the following bones make up the ankle?

a. Talus, fibula, tibia
b. Fibula, tarsal, talus
c. Metatarsal, tibia, cuboid
d. Navicular, fibula, tibia

59. Which internationally recognized pictogram might be found on the label of a skin irritant?

a. Exclamation mark
b. Skull and crossbones
c. Flame over circle
d. Flame

60. Out of the following choices, which nail product is capable of harboring bacteria or pathogens?

a. Nail polish
b. Nail polish remover
c. Cuticle softener
d. Acetone

61. Which segment of the hair strand is impacted by a direct dye?

a. The cuticle
b. The cortex
c. The medulla
d. The entire strand

62. A nail that is discolored should not be polished because _____.

a. Discoloration can cause the polish to look different.
b. Discoloration will cause the polish to chip away.
c. Discoloration may be the result of an underlying condition.
d. Discoloration is likely caused by residual nail polish, which should be removed first.

63. What does OSHA stand for?

a. Occupational State and Health Association
b. Occupational Safety and Health Association
c. Occupational System and Health Association
d. Occupational Safety and Health Administration

64. Which of the following conditions would be a contraindication for a nail service?

a. Onychocryptosis
b. Onychoptosis
c. Onychauxis
d. Onychophagy

65. Tina's extensions get tangled and matted easily, so she is in the market for a new brand. What characteristic should she look for in her new hair extensions to avoid this problem?

    a. Synthetic
    b. Human
    c. Remy
    d. Straight

66. _____ is an ingredient sometimes contained in topical skin-care products, and its use is a contraindication for depilatory treatment.

    a. Alpha hydroxyl acid
    b. Cetyl alcohol
    c. Tocopherol
    d. Butylene glycol

67. This brush has a large, flat base.

    a. Paddle brush
    b. Vent brush
    c. Grooming brush
    d. Teasing brush

68. What is the definition of PPE?

    a. Protective proactive equipment
    b. Proper protective equipment
    c. Protective personal equipment
    d. Personal protective equipment

69. Marnie is a lawyer who does a lot of typing. Which nail shape would be advisable for her profession?

    a. Squoval
    b. Round
    c. Oval
    d. Square

70. Which of the following tools is recommended for creating straight lines while sectioning hair?

    a. A tail comb
    b. A cutting/styling comb
    c. A paddle brush
    d. A teasing comb

71. A solution contains an excess of negatively charged hydroxide ions. Which of the following pH balances would the solution be most likely to have?

    a. 3
    b. 4.5-5.5
    c. 10
    d. 7

72. How might a technician properly prepare an extraction tool for reuse?

    a. Submerge in an EPA-registered disinfectant
    b. Thoroughly clean off debris with 90% alcohol
    c. Submerge in an EPA-registered sterilant
    d. Thoroughly clean off debris with an EPA-registered disinfectant

73. _____ shampoo is recommended for hair that has been color treated.

    a. Tinted
    b. Chelating
    c. Protein-rich
    d. pH-balanced

74. Runners who wear tight shoes may be susceptible to which of the following?

    a. Koilonychia
    b. Splinter hemorrhage
    c. Onychocryptosis
    d. Onychia

75. The following procedure should be used when filing nails:

    a. From the center of the nail to the outer edge.
    b. Back and forth in smooth, even strokes.
    c. From the outer edge to the center of the nail.
    d. In one direction at a time, with smooth and even strokes.

76. Out of the following colors listed, which roller will create the softest flow and movement?

    a. Yellow
    b. Blue
    c. Orange
    d. Red

77. Michelle's hair has not been cut in six months and her ends are tangling. Which of the following conditions might cause this to happen?

    a. Monilethrix
    b. Hypertrichosis
    c. Malassezia
    d. Trichoptilosis

78. Which of the following statements is true regarding head lice?

    a. Head lice can spread by jumping from one host to another.
    b. Hairstylists should be able to identify and diagnose the presence of head lice.
    c. Presence of lice eggs (nits) would be considered an infectious stage of the life cycle of head lice
    d. Hair color or hair bleach will kill head lice.

79. _____ is the last area on which a thio-based relaxer should be applied.

    a. The occipital
    b. The nape
    c. The hairline
    d. The roots

80. How many involuntary systems make up the circulatory system?
    a. Four
    b. Two
    c. Six
    d. Three

81. _____ is a skin conditioner that adds moisture to the skin, resulting in a smoother texture.
    a. Glyceryl monostearate
    b. Butylene glycol
    c. DMDM hydantoin
    d. Isopropyl lanolate

82. In the event that nail glue accidentally causes the nail to become adhered to the skin, what would the proper course of action be?
    a. Wait until the glue dries and carefully separate the skin from the nail
    b. Remove the dry glue from the skin with a nail file or buffer
    c. Separate the skin from the nail while the glue is still wet and remove excess glue with an orangewood stick
    d. Remove the nail glue by utilizing an acetone-soaked piece of cotton on the end of an orangewood stick

83. What is the proper draping for a demi-permanent hair color service?
    a. Use of a chemical cape
    b. Use of a towel, layered with a chemical cape
    c. Use of a towel, layered with a cloth cape, followed by a towel on top
    d. Use of a towel, layered with a chemical cape, followed by a towel on top

84. What is being extracted from the skin during the extraction process of a facial service?
    a. Pus, or white blood cells
    b. Bacteria
    c. Sebum
    d. Dead skin cells

85. _____ is the name of the muscle located in front of the ear.
    a. Procerus anterior
    b. Auricularis anterior
    c. Auricularis superior
    d. Frontalis

86. Which of the following conditions of the skin would be known as a communicable affliction?
    a. Dermatitis
    b. Eczema
    c. Folliculitis
    d. Impetigo

87. Which of the following muscles is responsible for separating the fingers?

    a. Abductor
    b. Opponens
    c. Adductor
    d. Abductor hallucis

88. What technique is most effective in keeping a patron's back dry during a shampoo service?

    a. Using a plastic cape
    b. Placing the cape behind the shampoo chair
    c. Putting a towel between the shampoo bowl and patron
    d. Letting the stream of water flow away from the patron's face

89. What is the most accurate method for testing the porosity of hair?

    a. Saturating with water and letting it air dry
    b. Stretching the hair strand and measuring its ability to return to its original length
    c. Testing the hair's ability to backcomb
    d. Utilizing varying degrees of heat to dry the hair

90. Which of the following areas of the head contains the LEAST amount of pigment?

    a. The front hairline
    b. The top of the head
    c. Below the occipital bone
    d. At the parietal ridge

91. Within a nail service, which of the following would be an example of a single-use or disposable tool?

    a. A nail brush
    b. A plastic spatula
    c. An orangewood stick
    d. A nail trimmer

92. If an air bubble is noticed within wet nail glue or under a nail enhancement, what course of action should be taken?

    a. Carefully pierce the bubble's surface and apply more glue
    b. No action is necessary
    c. Remove the nail and begin again
    d. Push the nail down firmly onto the nailbed to release the trapped air

93. Which of the following is an example of a non-communicable disease?

    a. Verruca
    b. Psoriasis
    c. Conjunctivitis
    d. Impetigo

94. A fine-grit nail file is used for _____.

a. Creating shine on the nail plate
b. Smoothing out roughness on the free edge
c. Removing length from the free edge
d. Removing dried polish from the skin

95. This portion of the pin curl is secured in place with a single- or double-pronged clip.

a. Stem
b. Base
c. Circle
d. Arc

96. Which of the following statements is uniquely true for Velcro rollers?

a. They are used on wet hair
b. They create volume
c. They come in different colors
d. They do not require clips

97. Jessica is under a great deal of stress. As a result of this, she is losing a lot of hair. What phase of hair growth causes this?

a. Anagen
b. Androgen
c. Telogen
d. Catagen

98. There are two parts to both a perm and a relaxer service, known as the physical stage and the chemical stage. The physical stage in a permanent wave is the wrapping of the hair around the rod. What is the physical stage in a relaxer service?

a. Applying the relaxer
b. Combing the hair
c. Applying the neutralizer
d. Smoothing the hair

99. Which of the following colors of rollers is the smallest in size?

a. Yellow
b. Blue
c. Red
d. Orange

100. Within the hair follicle, which component is re-formed during a permanent wave or relaxer service?

a. Salt bond
b. Disulfide bond
c. Hydrogen bond
d. Van der Waals force peptide chain

Answer Key and Explanations

1. B: The pH of skin and hair is between 4.5 and 5.5. In the event that the skin's pH becomes unbalanced, characteristics such as redness, dryness, and a chafed look may appear. The skin may be rebalanced by applying a product such as a toner, which would then aid in restoring the smooth texture of "normalized" skin.

2. C: Galvanic current can be used to provide desincrustation of hardened sebum found in hair follicles. Galvanic current utilizes two poles of current: the positively charged anode and the negatively charged cathode. The desincrustation process utilizes the cathode as the "active" pole, transmitting electric current through an alkaline substance, which in turn breaks down the sebum.

3. A: Prednisone, a steroid treatment, can cause the skin to thin. Thinner skin is more fragile and can become damaged easily. A spa client should not receive a facial service while taking prednisone or any other form of steroid treatment.

4. A: Onychatrophia can be caused either by sustaining an injury to the nail or a systemic disease. In cases of systemic disease, the nail may not return to its original state. With injury-related onychatrophia, the nail may improve in three to six months. If this condition is present, service should not be rendered to the nail.

5. B: Scabies is characterized by red, itchy, and watery blisters. The fact that the blisters are watery is a key indicator. Scabies is an infectious parasitic disorder caused by itch mites burrowing under the skin. Patrons displaying symptoms should not be serviced but instead referred to a physician for proper diagnosis.

6. A: Nail polish remover has a pH range of 5-6. Nail polish remover is alkaline in nature. This is important to know because alkaline substances can cause nails to become brittle and dry.

7. C: A sloughing lotion is used to remove dead skin cells from the feet during a pedicure. Most sloughing lotions contain a chemical exfoliant and require friction to work effectively.

8. A: A pH meter is the most accurate way to determine the pH of a product because it can be used to determine the exact pH of a substance. Another use of a pH meter is to determine the strength and accuracy of old developers.

9. C: The papilla supplies nourishment to the surrounding germinal matrix cells, which is where cell division ultimately takes place. Although hair itself is not a living thing, its growth is dependent on the type of nourishment supplied by an individual's body. It is for this reason that diet, medication, and other body conditions have been known to affect a person's hair growth and overall quality.

10. B: A Dutch braid is used to create cornrow braids. A Dutch braid is created in a similar manner to a French braid, with the exception of weaving the three strands under each other rather than over. A traditional cornrow style is a look that is created by using multiple narrow sub-sections to create narrow Dutch braids that sit closely to the head.

11. A: Amines/quats smooth the outside layer of the hair, or cuticle. If a raised cuticle is present, friction against other raised cuticles can create static and cause the hair to tangle.

---

12. D: The tang is the part of a razor or shears located on the finger hole of the cutting blade, or at the end of a razor. This part of the tool allows the technician balance and adds additional force when maneuvering.

13. D: Ammonium hydroxide is a derivative of thioglycolic acid, the main ingredient in alkaline waves. The swelling function of the ammonium hydroxide allows the thioglycolic acid to penetrate into the hair follicle. This is necessary in order to break the disulfide bonds so that hair can then be re-formed into a new shape.

14. D: A Wood's lamp is used in a facial to provide the technician with ultraviolet light. This special type of light allows for a specialized view of the deeper layers of the skin, which can be helpful in identifying conditions such as sun damage.

15. D: Comedo (plural: comedones) is the technical name for a blackhead. Blackheads are very common and occur when excess oil and/or dry skin cells cause a pore to become clogged.

16. C: A wooden nail file falls into the classification of disposable because it is a porous substance. Only non-porous substances can be disinfected or sterilized. In the event that a disposable implement should come into contact with blood, it should be double-bagged and disposed of in a manner compliant with the local regulations agency.

17. B: The nail matrix is located at the base of the nail, invisible to sight. Within the nail matrix, cell generation takes place. These cells harden over time, ultimately resulting in the hardened free edge of the nail.

18. B: Scalp massage stimulates the scalp, which in turn increases blood flow to the papilla. Increased blood flow to the papilla provides nourishment, which is necessary for hair growth.

19. C: A graduated technique, often referred to as graduation, occurs when hair is cut gradually from long to short. Graduation results in the creation of bulk and is often used in the nape of a short haircut, creating bulk towards the occipital.

20. C: While all options listed are capable of altering the tone of the hair, temporary hair color is the only option listed that would not chemically alter or damage the hair.

21. A: It takes 25-30 days for skin cells to complete the process of keratinization. Skin is comprised of five layers, and the process of keratinization, or shedding of the skin, takes place in the stratum corneum (uppermost) layer of the skin.

22. A: In the forming of acrylic nails, the middle of the nail should contain the thickest layer of acrylic. The thick area of acrylic in the middle area of the nail provides strength to the nail and support to the free edge.

23. D: Sterilization is the highest form of infection control used in a salon/spa, as well as hospital settings. Sterilization can be achieved by submerging tools in a liquid sterilant or with use of moist or dry heat at a high setting. Sterilization can only be achieved on non-porous surfaces.

24. C: "Cutting past the second knuckle" interferes with the outcome of the hair design because it causes the hair strand to lack the tension required for an accurate result. The tension on the hair provided by the area up to the first knuckle is greater and results in even tension.

25. B: Intensity is a term used to describe the vibrancy of a pigment. In this context, intensity describes tones of red in hair color.

26. B: Nail ridges should be eliminated by use of a fine-grit nail file followed by a nail buffer. Medium-grit nail files and mechanical files pose the risk of removing too much of the nail plate and should not be used. In the event that the client has deeper ridges, a ridge filler can be used.

27. A: A chelating shampoo removes surface and chemical buildup. Thoroughly cleansed hair is necessary for the permanent wave solution to penetrate into the hair follicle. Buildup of surface contaminates can inhibit the effectiveness of the perm.

28. C: To create curls on clean, dry hair, a Marcel iron would be the best choice. The other options listed require the hair to be wet.

29. C: Keratin is often used in strengthening shampoos. Hair that is dry and brittle often contains breakage and may require strengthening. A shampoo containing keratin or another protein complex might be recommended for consistent use prior to a chemical service.

30. B: Hair color lightening is caused by the diffusion of pigment within the hair follicle. This breaking down of the pigment of the hair creates smaller particles that allow the light to pass through the hair more readily, thus creating the visual appearance of lighter hair.

31. D: Determining the acidity of a substance can help you to anticipate how it might influence the skin, hair, or nail that you apply it to.

32. A: In theory, contouring draws the eye away from the feature by using a shade darker than its surrounding shade. When used in conjunction with highlighting, it can create a new shape to a facial feature by visually minimizing (contouring) certain aspects and enhancing (highlighting) other aspects.

33. A: Exfoliation is a great way to help minimize eczema flare-ups. Proper exfoliation will help to remove dead skin cells on the surface of the skin, allowing steroidal or other treatments to penetrate most effectively. Special caution should be taken to NOT over-exfoliate eczematic skin, because doing so can cause damage to the skin's surface and allow bacteria to enter.

34. D: The most effective practice of infection control is the use of disposable implements, specifically those used to pierce the skin. Disposable lancets or needles should be disposed of in a sealed, closed container labeled in accordance with the local regulating agency.

35. A: One of the benefits of using vibration in a facial service is that it can increase muscle tone. One contributing factor to this end result is an increase in blood circulation, providing nourishment to the area of application.

36. B: The function of a razor includes a replaceable blade. Any variety of shears (i.e., thinning shears, standard shears) are generally made to be sharpened. The blade of some mechanical tools, such as a clipper or neck trimmer, are also capable of being sharpened or replaced.

37. D: Any topical product used by a cosmetologist should be done in accordance with manufacturer's directions. In this case, different callus removers call for their own specifications (i.e., wet and/or dry skin) and may require specific direction effectiveness.

38. C: Disinfection is the mid-level form of infection control used in salon and spa settings. The purpose of a disinfectant is to remove dirt and kill certain bacteria on non-porous surfaces. Sterilization is the only method of infection control that can kill bacterial spores.

39. C: A blending shear has the greatest number of teeth out of all of the shears used for texturizing, and is capable of removing the greatest amount of bulk.

40. D: Emulsifier comes from the root word emulsion. An example of an emulsion would be oil and water. An emulsifier in shampoo is important because it helps the water (applied in the shampooing process) and oil (contained within a head of hair) bond together and wash away.

41. C: When changing the shape of the hair using a thermal tool, higher heat settings are often needed with coarse/curly hair. Hair that is coarse/curly generally has a larger diameter and requires a higher heat setting to achieve desired results. A good rule of thumb is to start with a lower heat setting and increase it as needed.

42. C: Hair color should be applied to the hair after a relaxer or perm to minimize color fading. The hair color molecules used to color hair can be deposited under the surface of the hair's cuticle. The chemical process of perming or relaxing the hair involves lifting the cuticle, which can allow the color molecules to escape, which can result in fading. Many perms also contain a chemical reaction similar to that of hydrogen peroxide and can cause even the natural pigment in a client's hair to lighten.

43. A: Washing the affected area with soap and water should be the first step a technician takes if they cut themselves. Washing with soap and water will remove debris and surface microbes that might readily enter an open wound.

44. B: The technical name for holding the closed shears away from the client in the palm of the hand is known as palming. Palming is a technique used during haircuts to minimize the potential contamination of the shears caused by putting them down. Palming the shears allows the technician to hold the shears safely while still having use of the remaining fingers to maneuver the hair.

45. B: In order to provide beneficial application while minimizing the likelihood of burns, a facial steamer should be used 16-18 inches from the client's face. Proper ventilation also ensures the effectiveness of the mist from a steamer.

46. B: A clay-based mask can be used during a facial to temporarily reduce the appearance of large pores. Often used on oil-rich skin, a clay-based mask is capable of absorbing excess oil and sebum, resulting in the appearance of smaller pores.

47. D: Fine hair is most susceptible to static electricity because it is often missing the medulla, which otherwise contributes to the overall weight of the hair strand.

48. A: Permanent hair color is the only variety of hair color capable of completely covering gray hair. While lightening the natural hair color is possible with permanent hair color, it is not a necessary function when gray hair coverage is desired.

49. A: Onychogryphosis is a systemic condition that causes an increased thickness and/or curvature of the nail. It can be caused by injury to the nail or old age. Onychogryphosis is often found within the big toenail and can make the nail difficult to trim and keep clean. It is recommended that trimming of a nail with onychogryphosis be done by a podiatrist.

50. A: Paronychia is a bacterial infection, found around the skin of the nail, that causes the affected skin to be swollen and warm to the touch. Clients who are experiencing these symptoms should be referred to a physician.

51. D: Use of bleach as a submersion liquid can corrode tools. Immersion in a broad-spectrum disinfectant is the best choice for shears that have come into contact with blood. The CDC guidelines state that a diluted bleach solution can be used to clean hard surfaces in the event that there is no other substitute.

52. D: The purpose of a waving lotion in any perm is to break down the structure of the hair for re-forming. An exothermic perm is unique in that it relies on an outside heat source to penetrate into the hair strand.

53. A: Rosacea is a chronic inflammatory congestion of the skin often found on the nose and cheeks. The characteristic redness is caused by broken capillaries visible on the skin's surface. In cases of acne rosacea, this redness can sometimes be accompanied by papules or pustules. Spicy foods and alcoholic beverages have been known to exasperate the redness, as can the application of topical irritants such as perfume. Clients experiencing rosacea can receive facial services only with the approval of a physician.

54. B: The proper positioning of the arch of the eyebrow can be determined by using the iris as a point of reference. This can be done with a client looking straight ahead and envisioning a line going directly up to the eyebrow.

55. B: A stylist's hands are capable of cross-contaminating the greatest number of surfaces in a salon/spa. Proper and frequent handwashing greatly lessens the spread of harmful bacteria.

56. B: A chin-length bob minimizes the look of a long face by bringing attention to the chin. Hair cut at the collar bone or in any sort of lob (long bob) further elongates the face. A pixie cut would be a static, non-moving hairstyle that would also emphasize any face shape.

57. D: Slithering is a technique done with shears. In this process, the open shears are moved in an up and down motion along the hair strands. Slithering is used to create texture or remove bulk from the hair.

58. A: The ankle joint forms where the fibula and tibia (lower leg bones) meet with the talus, or anklebone.

59. A: An exclamation mark is the pictogram found on the label of a skin irritant. Pictograms are internationally used to identify ingredients in a substance that may cause harm to the user.

60. C: Cuticle-softening products are capable of harboring bacteria and pathogens. For this reason, special care should be taken to apply cuticle softener without the bottle or dropper coming into direct contact with either the client or the technician's skin.

61. A: A direct dye works by directly staining the cuticle of the hair. Direct dyes can also be found as additives in permanent hair color to enhance the end tonal result. Presence of a direct dye can often be indicated by the resulting color being visually present in the hair color itself. For instance, if the direct dye is intended to color the hair purple, the color itself will be purple.

62. C: Discoloration in a nail may be the sign of an underlying condition, so discolored nails should not be serviced. For example, a nail that has a mustard yellow tint to it may be affected by nail fungus, which is a communicable disorder.

Clients with nail discoloration of any variety should be referred to a physician.

63. D: OSHA, or the Occupational Safety and Health Administration, is a division of the Department of Labor. It is a regulatory agency that enforces health and safety standards in the workplace.

64. B: Onychoptosis is defined as the shedding or falling off of a nail, and no service should be performed on the affected nail. Onychoptosis can be injury- or disease-related and should be referred to a physician.

65. C: Remy hair is the term used for hair extensions in which the hair strands are laid individually in the same direction from scalp to ends, as would be found in natural hair. When the hair strands are placed in alternate directions or opposite directions, this causes the cuticles of each strand to become tangled with one another.

66. A: Alpha hydroxyl acid is an exfoliant contained in many skin care products. Exfoliants are commonly utilized to smooth wrinkles or help prevent acne by removing dead skin cells from the surface of the skin. Clients using exfoliants may be lacking this protective barrier of the skin, and so should not receive depilatory services.

67. A: The paddle brush has a large, flat, and often square base. A paddle brush is best used on medium to long lengths for detangling or when smoothing hair with a blow dryer.

68. D: Personal protective equipment is defined by OSHA as "a specialized clothing or equipment worn by an employee for protection against a hazard." In addition to lessening the degree of cross-contamination in the workplace, PPE is also used to protect the technician from harmful inhalants such as carcinogens or topical irritants.

69. A: Squoval is a term used to describe a square shape that is rounded at the corners. It is ideal for professions where work with the hands is frequent.

70. A: A tail comb is most effective in creating straight lines while sectioning the hair. A tail comb can be identified by a narrow, straight end with no teeth.

71. C: The amount of positively or negatively charged ions in a substance is what determines its pH measurement. A solution that is more acidic has more positively charged (H^+) ions, whereas a substance with an alkaline measurement would have more negatively charged (OH^-) ions.

72. A: Tools used for extraction must be submerged in an EPA-registered disinfectant following the removal of debris. Said disinfectant must be registered as effective against HIV, human hepatitis B, and tuberculosis.

73. D: A pH-balanced shampoo will help to minimize the damage caused by alkaline-containing chemical services such as color or perms. A low-pH shampoo will help to close the cuticle of the hair, resulting in additional shine. It also adds longevity to the perm and color.

74. B: Splinter hemorrhage is another term for a bruised nail. In this condition, bruising occurs when broken capillaries cause blood to be trapped under the nail. In the event of a client with a bruised nail, special care should be taken to avoid pressure on the top of the nail. There is no treatment for a bruised nail other than time because the bruise will grow out with the nail.

75. C: Nails should be filed from the outer edge to the center of the nail. This technique allows filing to take place without putting unnecessary strain on the nail.

76. D: Red rollers are the biggest rollers of the colors listed, and are capable of creating the softest flow and volume. The smaller the roller, the more static (non-moving) the resulting shape becomes, prohibiting flow of the hair.

77. D: Trichoptilosis of the hair, otherwise known as split ends, can be caused by heat or other environmental stressors over the course of time. Use of a conditioner can smooth the cuticle, therefore minimizing the characteristics of trichoptilosis.

78. C: In the event that nits OR lice are present in a client's hair, there is a chance of further contamination. Nits are technically clear in color, but may appear to be white in darker hair. A louse nit is firmly affixed to the base of the hair follicle. Nits are most often found in the base of the head or behind the ear. Adult lice move by crawling. They are incapable or jumping or flying. If a stylist identifies what appears to be nits, they should refer a client to a doctor for a proper diagnosis.

79. C: Due to the fragile state of hair found at the hairline, any type of relaxer should be applied in this area last. Hair found at the hairline is often most impacted by face washing and other environmental factors, which contribute to its fragility.

80. B: There are two systems that make up the circulatory system, and both are involuntary. The two systems are the cardiovascular (blood vascular system) and lymph vascular system. These systems are responsible for circulating the blood and lymphatic fluid throughout the body.

81. D: Isopropyl lanolate can serve as a moisturizer or as an emulsifier. Maintaining a healthy moisture balance is important because it strengthens the skin's surface, which acts as a barrier against bacteria.

82. C: Careful placement is essential when using nail glue near the skin. In the event that glue does get on the skin, it is best to separate the skin from the nail when the glue is still wet and remove additional glue.

83. D: Chemical services require the layering of a towel, followed by a chemical cape, followed by another towel layered on top. During any chemical service, proper draping helps to ensure that the chemicals do not come into contact with a patron's skin or clothing. Chemical capes are made of plastic, which is made to be unabsorbent.

84. C: Sebum is extracted from the skin during an extraction procedure. Sebum is the oil naturally secreted by the skin, which provides hydration as well as a moisture barrier for the skin. Sebum can harden over time and clog the hair shaft and pores of the skin, potentially resulting in a stretching of the pores or even an infection.

85. B: There are three muscles that surround the ear. Each muscle name begins with the word auricularis, which stems from the word auricle (ear). The location of each muscle is further identified with the Latin names for front, above, and behind.

86. D: Impetigo is a highly communicable (contagious) affliction, caused by the staphylococcus bacteria entering the body by way of broken skin. Impetigo causes itchiness and presents itself by the presence of a yellowish crusted lesion on the skin's surface.

87. A: One abductor muscle can be found between each finger, where the finger meets the hand. The abductor is responsible for separating the fingers, whereas the similarly named adductor is responsible for drawing the fingers together.

112

88. B: Putting the cape behind the chair will encourage any accidental water flow to run down the cape, rather than down the back of the patron.

89. C: Hair that is porous will have the greatest ability to backcomb and remain in its new shape. Hair that is healthy and uncompromised possesses a smooth surface that will not readily hold a backcombed shape.

90. A: Hair located at the hairline contains the LEAST amount of pigment. This is important to know because hair with less pigment will lighten more easily. In some cases, an alternate formula may be necessary in order to create an evenly colored end result.

91. C: An orangewood stick is an example of a single-use or disposable tool. Any item with a porous composition is unable to be sanitized, and therefore should be labeled as disposable.

92. D: In the event that an air bubble is visible underneath a nail enhancement, press the nail down firmly onto the nailbed to release the trapped air. If the glue has already hardened, the enhancement must be removed and reapplied.

93. B: A non-communicable disease is a disease that cannot be transmitted from one person to another. Salon professionals should NOT perform services if a communicable disease is present; instead, the salon client should be referred to a physician.

94. B: A fine-grit nail file is used to smooth rough edges of the free edge of the nail. Due to its low-volume grit surface, it is capable of smoothing rough edges.

95. B: The base of the hair is the portion of the pin curl that is affixed to the scalp area. Improper positioning of the clip can result in clip marks in the curl.

96. D: Velcro rollers are unique in that they do not require clips in order to adhere to the hair. Velcro rollers have tiny C-shaped teeth that hold on to the hair. All of the other characteristics listed are true of Velcro rollers, but the fact that they do not require clips is what makes Velcro rollers unique.

97. C: There are three phases of hair growth: anagen, catagen, and telogen. The telogen phase is the final phase of the hair growth process, during which time the root sheath, which affixes the hair in place on the scalp, is no longer attached. Without the root sheath present, the hair falls out.

98. D: The smoothing of the hair is the physical stage of a relaxer service. Smoothing of the hair takes place after application of the relaxer product. The smoothing process involves running the back of the comb against the head (or hair, if length is present) to form a modified, straight position.

99. B: Blue is the smallest roller of the options listed. Blue rollers are used on short hair, often in the nape of a hairstyle. These small rollers are capable of creating the greatest amount of volume.

100. B: During a perm or chemical relaxer service, the disulfide bonds of the hair are broken and then re-formed into a new shape. A waving lotion or relaxing product is responsible for the breaking of the disulfide bonds, whereas a neutralizer re-forms them.

How to Overcome Test Anxiety

Just the thought of taking a test is enough to make most people a little nervous. A test is an important event that can have a long-term impact on your future, so it's important to take it seriously and it's natural to feel anxious about performing well. But just because anxiety is normal, that doesn't mean that it's helpful in test taking, or that you should simply accept it as part of your life. Anxiety can have a variety of effects. These effects can be mild, like making you feel slightly nervous, or severe, like blocking your ability to focus or remember even a simple detail.

If you experience test anxiety—whether severe or mild—it's important to know how to beat it. To discover this, first you need to understand what causes test anxiety.

Causes of Test Anxiety

While we often think of anxiety as an uncontrollable emotional state, it can actually be caused by simple, practical things. One of the most common causes of test anxiety is that a person does not feel adequately prepared for their test. This feeling can be the result of many different issues such as poor study habits or lack of organization, but the most common culprit is time management. Starting to study too late, failing to organize your study time to cover all of the material, or being distracted while you study will mean that you're not well prepared for the test. This may lead to cramming the night before, which will cause you to be physically and mentally exhausted for the test. Poor time management also contributes to feelings of stress, fear, and hopelessness as you realize you are not well prepared but don't know what to do about it.

Other times, test anxiety is not related to your preparation for the test but comes from unresolved fear. This may be a past failure on a test, or poor performance on tests in general. It may come from comparing yourself to others who seem to be performing better or from the stress of living up to expectations. Anxiety may be driven by fears of the future—how failure on this test would affect your educational and career goals. These fears are often completely irrational, but they can still negatively impact your test performance.

> **Review Video: 3 Reasons You Have Test Anxiety**
> Visit mometrix.com/academy and enter code: 428468

Elements of Test Anxiety

As mentioned earlier, test anxiety is considered to be an emotional state, but it has physical and mental components as well. Sometimes you may not even realize that you are suffering from test anxiety until you notice the physical symptoms. These can include trembling hands, rapid heartbeat, sweating, nausea, and tense muscles. Extreme anxiety may lead to fainting or vomiting. Obviously, any of these symptoms can have a negative impact on testing. It is important to recognize them as soon as they begin to occur so that you can address the problem before it damages your performance.

Review Video: 3 Ways to Tell You Have Test Anxiety
Visit mometrix.com/academy and enter code: 927847

The mental components of test anxiety include trouble focusing and inability to remember learned information. During a test, your mind is on high alert, which can help you recall information and stay focused for an extended period of time. However, anxiety interferes with your mind's natural processes, causing you to blank out, even on the questions you know well. The strain of testing during anxiety makes it difficult to stay focused, especially on a test that may take several hours. Extreme anxiety can take a huge mental toll, making it difficult not only to recall test information but even to understand the test questions or pull your thoughts together.

Review Video: How Test Anxiety Affects Memory
Visit mometrix.com/academy and enter code: 609003

Effects of Test Anxiety

Test anxiety is like a disease—if left untreated, it will get progressively worse. Anxiety leads to poor performance, and this reinforces the feelings of fear and failure, which in turn lead to poor performances on subsequent tests. It can grow from a mild nervousness to a crippling condition. If allowed to progress, test anxiety can have a big impact on your schooling, and consequently on your future.

Test anxiety can spread to other parts of your life. Anxiety on tests can become anxiety in any stressful situation, and blanking on a test can turn into panicking in a job situation. But fortunately, you don't have to let anxiety rule your testing and determine your grades. There are a number of relatively simple steps you can take to move past anxiety and function normally on a test and in the rest of life.

Review Video: How Test Anxiety Impacts Your Grades
Visit mometrix.com/academy and enter code: 939819

Physical Steps for Beating Test Anxiety

While test anxiety is a serious problem, the good news is that it can be overcome. It doesn't have to control your ability to think and remember information. While it may take time, you can begin taking steps today to beat anxiety.

Just as your first hint that you may be struggling with anxiety comes from the physical symptoms, the first step to treating it is also physical. Rest is crucial for having a clear, strong mind. If you are tired, it is much easier to give in to anxiety. But if you establish good sleep habits, your body and mind will be ready to perform optimally, without the strain of exhaustion. Additionally, sleeping well helps you to retain information better, so you're more likely to recall the answers when you see the test questions.

Getting good sleep means more than going to bed on time. It's important to allow your brain time to relax. Take study breaks from time to time so it doesn't get overworked, and don't study right before bed. Take time to rest your mind before trying to rest your body, or you may find it difficult to fall asleep.

> **Review Video: The Importance of Sleep for Your Brain**
> Visit mometrix.com/academy and enter code: 319338

Along with sleep, other aspects of physical health are important in preparing for a test. Good nutrition is vital for good brain function. Sugary foods and drinks may give a burst of energy but this burst is followed by a crash, both physically and emotionally. Instead, fuel your body with protein and vitamin-rich foods.

Also, drink plenty of water. Dehydration can lead to headaches and exhaustion, especially if your brain is already under stress from the rigors of the test. Particularly if your test is a long one, drink water during the breaks. And if possible, take an energy-boosting snack to eat between sections.

> **Review Video: How Diet Can Affect your Mood**
> Visit mometrix.com/academy and enter code: 624317

Along with sleep and diet, a third important part of physical health is exercise. Maintaining a steady workout schedule is helpful, but even taking 5-minute study breaks to walk can help get your blood pumping faster and clear your head. Exercise also releases endorphins, which contribute to a positive feeling and can help combat test anxiety.

When you nurture your physical health, you are also contributing to your mental health. If your body is healthy, your mind is much more likely to be healthy as well. So take time to rest, nourish your body with healthy food and water, and get moving as much as possible. Taking these physical steps will make you stronger and more able to take the mental steps necessary to overcome test anxiety.

Mental Steps for Beating Test Anxiety

Working on the mental side of test anxiety can be more challenging, but as with the physical side, there are clear steps you can take to overcome it. As mentioned earlier, test anxiety often stems from lack of preparation, so the obvious solution is to prepare for the test. Effective studying may be the most important weapon you have for beating test anxiety, but you can and should employ several other mental tools to combat fear.

First, boost your confidence by reminding yourself of past success—tests or projects that you aced. If you're putting as much effort into preparing for this test as you did for those, there's no reason you should expect to fail here. Work hard to prepare; then trust your preparation.

Second, surround yourself with encouraging people. It can be helpful to find a study group, but be sure that the people you're around will encourage a positive attitude. If you spend time with others who are anxious or cynical, this will only contribute to your own anxiety. Look for others who are motivated to study hard from a desire to succeed, not from a fear of failure.

Third, reward yourself. A test is physically and mentally tiring, even without anxiety, and it can be helpful to have something to look forward to. Plan an activity following the test, regardless of the outcome, such as going to a movie or getting ice cream.

When you are taking the test, if you find yourself beginning to feel anxious, remind yourself that you know the material. Visualize successfully completing the test. Then take a few deep, relaxing breaths and return to it. Work through the questions carefully but with confidence, knowing that you are capable of succeeding.

Developing a healthy mental approach to test taking will also aid in other areas of life. Test anxiety affects more than just the actual test—it can be damaging to your mental health and even contribute to depression. It's important to beat test anxiety before it becomes a problem for more than testing.

Review Video: <u>Test Anxiety and Depression</u>
Visit mometrix.com/academy and enter code: 904704

Study Strategy

Being prepared for the test is necessary to combat anxiety, but what does being prepared look like? You may study for hours on end and still not feel prepared. What you need is a strategy for test prep. The next few pages outline our recommended steps to help you plan out and conquer the challenge of preparation.

STEP 1: SCOPE OUT THE TEST

Learn everything you can about the format (multiple choice, essay, etc.) and what will be on the test. Gather any study materials, course outlines, or sample exams that may be available. Not only will this help you to prepare, but knowing what to expect can help to alleviate test anxiety.

STEP 2: MAP OUT THE MATERIAL

Look through the textbook or study guide and make note of how many chapters or sections it has. Then divide these over the time you have. For example, if a book has 15 chapters and you have five days to study, you need to cover three chapters each day. Even better, if you have the time, leave an extra day at the end for overall review after you have gone through the material in depth.

If time is limited, you may need to prioritize the material. Look through it and make note of which sections you think you already have a good grasp on, and which need review. While you are studying, skim quickly through the familiar sections and take more time on the challenging parts. Write out your plan so you don't get lost as you go. Having a written plan also helps you feel more in control of the study, so anxiety is less likely to arise from feeling overwhelmed at the amount to cover.

STEP 3: GATHER YOUR TOOLS

Decide what study method works best for you. Do you prefer to highlight in the book as you study and then go back over the highlighted portions? Or do you type out notes of the important information? Or is it helpful to make flashcards that you can carry with you? Assemble the pens, index cards, highlighters, post-it notes, and any other materials you may need so you won't be distracted by getting up to find things while you study.

If you're having a hard time retaining the information or organizing your notes, experiment with different methods. For example, try color-coding by subject with colored pens, highlighters, or post-it notes. If you learn better by hearing, try recording yourself reading your notes so you can listen while in the car, working out, or simply sitting at your desk. Ask a friend to quiz you from your flashcards, or try teaching someone the material to solidify it in your mind.

STEP 4: CREATE YOUR ENVIRONMENT

It's important to avoid distractions while you study. This includes both the obvious distractions like visitors and the subtle distractions like an uncomfortable chair (or a too-comfortable couch that makes you want to fall asleep). Set up the best study environment possible: good lighting and a comfortable work area. If background music helps you focus, you may want to turn it on, but otherwise keep the room quiet. If you are using a computer to take notes, be sure you don't have any other windows open, especially applications like social media, games, or anything else that could distract you. Silence your phone and turn off notifications. Be sure to keep water close by so you stay hydrated while you study (but avoid unhealthy drinks and snacks).

Also, take into account the best time of day to study. Are you freshest first thing in the morning? Try to set aside some time then to work through the material. Is your mind clearer in the afternoon or evening? Schedule your study session then. Another method is to study at the same time of day that you will take the test, so that your brain gets used to working on the material at that time and will be ready to focus at test time.

STEP 5: STUDY!

Once you have done all the study preparation, it's time to settle into the actual studying. Sit down, take a few moments to settle your mind so you can focus, and begin to follow your study plan. Don't give in to distractions or let yourself procrastinate. This is your time to prepare so you'll be ready to fearlessly approach the test. Make the most of the time and stay focused.

Of course, you don't want to burn out. If you study too long you may find that you're not retaining the information very well. Take regular study breaks. For example, taking five minutes out of every hour to walk briskly, breathing deeply and swinging your arms, can help your mind stay fresh.

As you get to the end of each chapter or section, it's a good idea to do a quick review. Remind yourself of what you learned and work on any difficult parts. When you feel that you've mastered the material, move on to the next part. At the end of your study session, briefly skim through your notes again.

But while review is helpful, cramming last minute is NOT. If at all possible, work ahead so that you won't need to fit all your study into the last day. Cramming overloads your brain with more information than it can process and retain, and your tired mind may struggle to recall even previously learned information when it is overwhelmed with last-minute study. Also, the urgent nature of cramming and the stress placed on your brain contribute to anxiety. You'll be more likely to go to the test feeling unprepared and having trouble thinking clearly.

So don't cram, and don't stay up late before the test, even just to review your notes at a leisurely pace. Your brain needs rest more than it needs to go over the information again. In fact, plan to finish your studies by noon or early afternoon the day before the test. Give your brain the rest of the day to relax or focus on other things, and get a good night's sleep. Then you will be fresh for the test and better able to recall what you've studied.

STEP 6: TAKE A PRACTICE TEST

Many courses offer sample tests, either online or in the study materials. This is an excellent resource to check whether you have mastered the material, as well as to prepare for the test format and environment.

Check the test format ahead of time: the number of questions, the type (multiple choice, free response, etc.), and the time limit. Then create a plan for working through them. For example, if you have 30 minutes to take a 60-question test, your limit is 30 seconds per question. Spend less time on the questions you know well so that you can take more time on the difficult ones.

If you have time to take several practice tests, take the first one open book, with no time limit. Work through the questions at your own pace and make sure you fully understand them. Gradually work up to taking a test under test conditions: sit at a desk with all study materials put away and set a timer. Pace yourself to make sure you finish the test with time to spare and go back to check your answers if you have time.

After each test, check your answers. On the questions you missed, be sure you understand why you missed them. Did you misread the question (tests can use tricky wording)? Did you forget the information? Or was it something you hadn't learned? Go back and study any shaky areas that the practice tests reveal.

Taking these tests not only helps with your grade, but also aids in combating test anxiety. If you're already used to the test conditions, you're less likely to worry about it, and working through tests until you're scoring well gives you a confidence boost. Go through the practice tests until you feel comfortable, and then you can go into the test knowing that you're ready for it.

Test Tips

On test day, you should be confident, knowing that you've prepared well and are ready to answer the questions. But aside from preparation, there are several test day strategies you can employ to maximize your performance.

First, as stated before, get a good night's sleep the night before the test (and for several nights before that, if possible). Go into the test with a fresh, alert mind rather than staying up late to study.

Try not to change too much about your normal routine on the day of the test. It's important to eat a nutritious breakfast, but if you normally don't eat breakfast at all, consider eating just a protein bar. If you're a coffee drinker, go ahead and have your normal coffee. Just make sure you time it so that the caffeine doesn't wear off right in the middle of your test. Avoid sugary beverages, and drink enough water to stay hydrated but not so much that you need a restroom break 10 minutes into the test. If your test isn't first thing in the morning, consider going for a walk or doing a light workout before the test to get your blood flowing.

Allow yourself enough time to get ready, and leave for the test with plenty of time to spare so you won't have the anxiety of scrambling to arrive in time. Another reason to be early is to select a good seat. It's helpful to sit away from doors and windows, which can be distracting. Find a good seat, get out your supplies, and settle your mind before the test begins.

When the test begins, start by going over the instructions carefully, even if you already know what to expect. Make sure you avoid any careless mistakes by following the directions.

Then begin working through the questions, pacing yourself as you've practiced. If you're not sure on an answer, don't spend too much time on it, and don't let it shake your confidence. Either skip it and come back later, or eliminate as many wrong answers as possible and guess among the remaining ones. Don't dwell on these questions as you continue—put them out of your mind and focus on what lies ahead.

Be sure to read all of the answer choices, even if you're sure the first one is the right answer. Sometimes you'll find a better one if you keep reading. But don't second-guess yourself if you do immediately know the answer. Your gut instinct is usually right. Don't let test anxiety rob you of the information you know.

If you have time at the end of the test (and if the test format allows), go back and review your answers. Be cautious about changing any, since your first instinct tends to be correct, but make sure you didn't misread any of the questions or accidentally mark the wrong answer choice. Look over any you skipped and make an educated guess.

At the end, leave the test feeling confident. You've done your best, so don't waste time worrying about your performance or wishing you could change anything. Instead, celebrate the successful completion of this test. And finally, use this test to learn how to deal with anxiety even better next time.

Review Video: 5 Tips to Beat Test Anxiety
Visit mometrix.com/academy and enter code: 570656

Important Qualification

Not all anxiety is created equal. If your test anxiety is causing major issues in your life beyond the classroom or testing center, or if you are experiencing troubling physical symptoms related to your anxiety, it may be a sign of a serious physiological or psychological condition. If this sounds like your situation, we strongly encourage you to seek professional help.

Tell Us Your Story

We at Mometrix would like to extend our heartfelt thanks to you for letting us be a part of your journey. It is an honor to serve people from all walks of life, people like you, who are committed to building the best future they can for themselves.

We know that each person's situation is unique. But we also know that, whether you are a young student or a mother of four, you care about working to make your own life and the lives of those around you better.

That's why we want to hear your story.

We want to know why you're taking this test. We want to know about the trials you've gone through to get here. And we want to know about the successes you've experienced after taking and passing your test.

In addition to your story, which can be an inspiration both to us and to others, we value your feedback. We want to know both what you loved about our book and what you think we can improve on.

The team at Mometrix would be absolutely thrilled to hear from you! So please, send us an email at tellusyourstory@mometrix.com or visit us at mometrix.com/tellusyourstory.php and let's stay in touch.

122

Additional Bonus Material

Due to our efforts to try to keep this book to a manageable length, we've created a link that will give you access to all of your additional bonus material.

Please visit http://www.mometrix.com/bonus948/cosmetology
to access the information.